The Neol

The Neoliberal Crisis

Edited by Sally Davison
& Katharine Harris

A SOUNDINGS COLLECTION

Soundings
A journal of politics and culture

London
Lawrence & Wishart 2015

Lawrence and Wishart Limited
99a Wallis Road
London
E9 5LN

Typesetting: e-type
Cover design: Andrew Corbett

ISBN 9781 910448 076

British Library Cataloguing in Publication Data.
A catalogue record for this book is available from the British Library

Published by Soundings

Soundings
A journal of politics and culture

CONTENTS

PREFACE

This volume brings together a range of articles originally published in *Soundings* between 2009 and 2011, and an introduction from the same moment. Each one remains relevant to the conjunctural discussion and analysis of neoliberalism that has consistently formed a substantial part of the work of *Soundings*. These articles are here re-released as a companion volume to the Kilburn Manifesto, to provide background and context to the Manifesto's more wide-ranging analysis.

Over the past decade, *Soundings* has sought to investigate how moments of crisis could offer the potential for disrupting the dominant consensus, and challenging the ideologies of neoliberalism. The introduction and articles in this collection engage with the renegotiations of the existing settlement that occurred in an effort to shore up neoliberal hegemony after the financial crisis in 2008.

At that time, the crisis appeared to have opened up a few cracks in the neoliberal structure – as both Doreen Massey and Michael Rustin write – and there was a small chance it might end up being buried by the weight of its own contradictions. But the crisis remained economic in nature: there was not an accompanying political challenge to the system. The drive to re-establish business as usual – as politicians have attempted to contain the crisis and have used it to justify the austerity agenda – is proving much more successful than might have been expected given the scale of system failure. The response to the crisis across Europe and North America, far from seeking a change in direction, has been to put in place measures to support the status quo, with banks being in receipt of huge amounts of state money, and financial support made available to keep the inflated property market buoyant, while the welfare state has been under attack, including through continuing privatisation within the public sector. These and other measures have led to the emergence of a stagnant, deflationary, low-waged economy in the UK, which has intersected with the financial and social travails of the Eurozone.

The Manifesto seeks to examine the underlying assumptions of neoliberalism in order to challenge them. Its aim is to call into question the neoliberal order and thus identify possible sites of political resistance. Republishing *The Neoliberal Crisis* articles as a complement to the Manifesto offers an opportunity to look to explore how this argument was developed as the crisis unfolded.

INTRODUCTION

The neoliberal revolution began in the 1970s, as an – extremely successful – attempt to roll back the gains of the post-war welfare state, reverse the gains of liberation movements and restore the dominance of business interests across the world. Over the last couple of years the editors of *Soundings* have been seeking to interpret these developments through the conceptual framework of conjunctural analysis, and this collection brings some of this ongoing work together, in the hope of aiding a wider understanding of what is at stake in our current political battles.

Stuart Hall has pioneered this way of writing about politics – based on analysing the contours of a given social, political and cultural conjuncture at a number of different levels. Following his seminal work on Thatcherism in the late 1970s and early 1980s, in recent years he has turned his attention to defining further phases within the neoliberal project – including an understanding of New Labour as a social-democratic variant of the work begun in Britain by Thatcherism.[1] He regards 'Cameronism' as the latest configuration of this neoliberal settlement.

In the first essay in this book, republished from *Soundings* 48, Stuart documents the processes of the neoliberal revolution, including the ancestral traditions from which it has drawn sustenance, and the different forms in which it has been incarnated in Britain – from Thatcher and Blair to its current heirs in the Coalition government.

Underpinning this analysis is the view that Thatcherism inaugurated a new conjunctural settlement, which can be described in short-hand terms as neoliberal. In this new social, cultural and political settlement, which replaced the previously existing post-war consensus, the notion that the market is the only way to organise society became the cultural bedrock of 'common sense'.

Stuart's article was part of a series of pieces that began with Mike Rustin's article in *Soundings* 43, published on the eve of the 2010 general election, which looked at the differences and similarities between the current financial crisis and the last major period of upheaval in British politics – the 1970s – when, after a period of struggle, Thatcherism defeated the left and put in place the current neoliberal settlement. The key difference Mike identifies is that the current crisis is the result of neoliberalism collapsing under its own contradictions; there has not been a major political battle with a strongly backed alternative to challenge dominant narratives. This weakness on the left is part of the bitter harvest of New Labour's inability to tackle vested interests and assert a social democratic leadership. New Labour actively enabled, or was content to preside over, the continuing destruction of the forces that might have been marshalled to challenge neoliberalism. This has made it all the more difficult to mobilise behind alternative solutions to the current financial collapse.

What we were seeing in the last days of New Labour were efforts by all the main political parties to address the current crisis through what John Clarke describes in his contribution (also first published in *Soundings* 43) as a 'restorationist' strategy. John argues that we are experiencing multiple crises, and multiple interpretations of those crises. There is intense competition 'to name the crisis, to identify its distinctive characteristics and treat it as the ground on which to demand new ways of doing things'. At the time of his article, the minimalist interpretation of what had gone wrong was prevailing: the main remedy on offer was a quick fix of the finance system before resuming business as usual. (It is still unclear whether or not Labour under Ed Miliband's leadership will be able to challenge this consensus, but he faces an uphill struggle. Cameron, on the other hand, while feeling the need to adopt a certain amount of critical language, seeks to avoid actually having to do anything. This is perhaps progress of a kind, but the dominant narrative today is of fiscal crisis rather than systemic financial crisis.)

As John also points out, the financial crisis requires a much more profound response than anything currently on offer. It represents the unravelling of many elements of the neoliberal settlement. And even if the 'restorationists' cobble together a short-term settlement – adjusted but not radically changed – they will not be able to resolve the problems of a global economy in meltdown. 2012's increasingly desperate attempts to save the euro are evidence of the truth of this argument.

The fourth chapter in this book, first published in *Soundings* 44, is a dialogue between Stuart Hall and Doreen Massey which elaborates more fully what is involved in conjunctural analysis: looking at the social, political, economic and cultural contradictions in any particular period of political settlement, and trying to understand how they are articulated to produce that settlement. A critical part of this kind of analysis is the recognition of the importance of culture. As Stuart argues, any serious analysis of the financial crisis must take into account its other 'conditions of existence'. The widespread acceptance of the centrality of market ways and market values is not something that relates only to the world of high finance; it is something that is culturally internalised by everyone; it is the common sense of the age.

It is partly through such common sense notions that hegemony is secured for a particular political project, class or interest. For political hegemony is much more than a temporary majority for a tactical programme; it implies a position of intellectual and moral leadership that can provide solutions for other classes and social groups, and unify them around a strategic vision and programme. Such a vision can be disrupted at moments of crisis – and indeed one reason for seeking to analyse such moments is to better understand how to politically intervene in the interests of an alternative hegemonic project.

But we will only succeed in opening up the debate on the alternatives by understanding that the economic agenda is itself part of a wider social and political settlement. As Doreen Massey reminded us in her essay first published in *Soundings* 45, there was a short moment, when the financial crisis first hit, when there appeared to be an opening up of new questions – about ways of being human, about ethics, about the wider hegemonic ideological framing of life. But since then the debate has been closed down again. Much work has been needed to bring us back on track, to return us to the idea that what is mainly needed is belt-tightening all round. But there are cracks in the consensus and we need to work to put forward the alternatives.

In his article first published in *Soundings* 48, Mike Rustin approaches these questions from the point of view of equilibrium: are there instabilities in the current settlement that mean it may be difficult to sustain? He argues that, like its forerunners in the neoliberal project, the current government has no answers to the problems of the British economy. Their strategy of cuts and rebalancing the economy towards the private sector will not succeed, and the problem for the Labour Party may lie not so much in pointing to the obvious weaknesses of government strategy, as in finding an alternative model for our economy and society that defeats the neoliberal revolutionaries and puts the well-being of the majority back at the heart of politics. This is, of course, an issue on which the whole of the left – including social movements, the trade unions and other civil society movements both new and old – needs to focus. And we need also to continue the search for creative ways of winning support for our alternatives.

As Doreen Massey argues in the final chapter of this book (also first published in *Soundings* 48), neoliberal ideology has remained more or less intact throughout the period of financial chaos we have been enduring. There is a sense of economic crisis but not the more profound questioning that would precipitate an ideological crisis. This is partly as a result of the huge amount of work the right always put in to secure consent for their hegemonic rule. Doreen argues that the left need to try to better understand the processes by which hegemony is created and maintained, and to find the most effective ways of challenging the dominant consensus, through establishing our own terrain, and thus bringing about a (re)definition of political frontiers. She also puts forward a number of suggested areas of engagement that could help us become clearer and sharper about what kind of society, and whose interests, we stand for.

NOTE

1. See, for example, 'New Labour's double shuffle', *Soundings* 24, Summer 2003.

1. THE NEOLIBERAL REVOLUTION

Stuart Hall

How do we make sense of our extraordinary political situation: the end of the debt-fuelled boom, the banking crisis of 2007-10, the defeat of New Labour and the rise to power of a Conservative-Liberal-Democratic Coalition? What sort of crisis is this? Is it a serious wobble in the trickle-down, win-win, end-of-boom-and-bust economic model which has dominated global capitalism? Does it presage business as usual, the deepening of present trends, or the mobilisation of social forces for a radical change of direction? Is this the start of a new conjuncture?

Gramsci argued that, though the economic must never be forgotten, conjunctural crises are never solely economic, or economically-determined 'in the last instance'. They arise when a number of contradictions at work in different key practices and sites come together – or 'conjoin' – in the same moment and political space and, as Althusser said, 'fuse in a ruptural unity'. Analysis here focuses on crises and breaks, and the distinctive character of the 'historic settlements' which follow. The condensation of forces during a period of crisis, and the new social configurations which result, mark a new 'conjuncture'.

My argument is that the present situation *is* a crisis, another unresolved rupture of that conjuncture which we can define as 'the long march of the Neoliberal Revolution'. Each crisis since the 1970s has looked different, arising from specific historical circumstances. However, they also seem to share some consistent underlying features, to be connected in their general thrust and direction of travel. Paradoxically, opposed political regimes have all contributed in different ways to expanding this project.

The term 'neoliberal' is not a satisfactory one. Its reference to the shaping influence of capitalism on modern life sounds recidivist to contemporary ears. Intellectual critics say the term lumps together too many things to merit a single identity; it is reductive, sacrificing attention to internal complexities and geohistorical specificity. I sympathise with this critique. However, I think there are enough common features to warrant giving it a *provisional* conceptual identity, provided this is understood as a first approximation. Even Marx argued that analysis yields understanding at different levels of abstraction, and critical thought often begins with a 'chaotic' abstraction – though we then need to add 'further determinations' in order to 'reproduce the concrete in thought'. I would also argue that naming neoliberalism is *politically* necessary, to give resistance content, focus and a cutting edge.

Pragmatism may account in part for this scepticism about neoliberalism as a concept: English intellectuals often cannot see the practical efficacy of long-term, theoretical ideas. A discussion on, say, the principles behind capital punishment quickly degenerates into a debate on whether hanging, drawing or quartering best achieves the purpose. I recall that many refused to apply the term 'project' to Thatcherism and New Labour, though it was crystal clear that neither political formation had been instituted by sleep-walkers, driven by purely pragmatic imperatives. But in English common sense, pragmatism often rules.

THE NEOLIBERAL MODEL

What, then, are the leading ideas of the neoliberal model? We can only pull at one thread here. However anachronistic it may seem, neoliberalism is grounded in the 'free, possessive individual', with the state cast as tyrannical and oppressive. The welfare state, in particular, is the arch enemy of freedom. The state must never govern society, dictate to free individuals how to dispose of their private property, regulate a free-market economy or interfere with the God-given right to make profits and amass personal wealth. State-led 'social engineering' must never prevail over corporate and private interests. It must not intervene in the 'natural' mechanisms of the free market, or take as its objective the amelioration of free-market capitalism's propensity to create inequality. Harvey's book offers a useful guide.[1] Theodore, Peck and Brenner summarise it thus: 'Open, competitive and unregulated markets, liberated from state intervention and the actions of social collectivities, represent the optimal mechanism to socio-economic development … This is the response of a revived capitalism to "the crisis of Keynesian welfarism" in the 70s'.[2] (Capitalism's other response, incidentally, was to evade state intervention by 'going global'.)

According to the neoliberal narrative, the welfare state (propelled by working-class reaction to the Depression of the 1930s and the popular mobilisation of World War Two) mistakenly saw its task as intervening in the economy, redistributing wealth, universalising life-chances, attacking unemployment, protecting the socially vulnerable, ameliorating the condition of oppressed or marginalised groups and addressing social injustice. It tried to break the 'natural' (sic) link between social needs and the individual's capacity to pay. But its do-gooding, utopian sentimentality enervated the nation's moral fibre, and eroded personal responsibility and the over-riding duty of the poor to work. It imposed social purposes on an economy rooted in individual greed and self interest. State intervention must never compromise the right of private capital to 'grow the business', improve share value, pay dividends and reward its agents with enormous salaries, benefits and bonuses. The function of the liberal state should be limited to safeguarding the conditions in which profitable competition can be pursued without engendering Hobbes's 'war of all against all'.

Margaret Thatcher, well instructed by Keith Joseph, grasped intuitively Hayek's argument that the 'common good' either did not exist or could not be calculated: 'There is no such thing as society. There is only the individual and his (sic) family'. She also grasped Milton Friedman's lesson that 'only a crisis – actual or perceived – produces real change. When that crisis occurs the actions that are taken depend on the ideas that are around … our basic function [is] to develop alternatives to existing policies … until the politically impossible becomes politically inevitable'.[3] As the free-market think-tank, the Institute of Economic Affairs, observed during the rise of Thatcherism, 'the market is an idea whose time has come'. This could well be a Coalition vision-statement.

The welfare state had made deep inroads into private capital's territory. To roll back that post-war 'settlement' and restore the prerogatives of capital had been the ambition of its opponents ever since Churchill dreamt in the 1950s of starting 'a bonfire of controls'. The crisis of the late 1960s-1970s was neoliberalism's opportunity, and the Thatcher and Reagan regimes grabbed it with both hands.

Neoliberalism is also critical to contemporary geopolitics. Structural adjustment programmes have forced the 'developing world' to set market forces free, and open their economies to free trade and foreign investment, while promoting the 'liberal' virtues of elections, multi-party politics, the rule of law and 'good governance'. This was the prescription to bring about the 'liberal-democracy' that Francis Fukayama saw as marking the end of ideology and the fulfilment of the struggle for the good life. Western super-powers have consistently intervened globally to defend this model in recent decades.

It should be noted, of course, that neoliberalism has many variants. There are critical differences, for example, between American, British and European 'social market' versions; South East Asian state-supported growth and Chinese 'state capitalism'; Russia's oligarchic/kleptomanic state and the monetarist 'experiments' in Latin America. Neoliberalism is not *one* thing. It evolves and diversifies. Nevertheless, geopolitically, neoliberal ideas, policies and strategies are incrementally gaining ground, re-defining the political, social and economic model, governing the strategies and setting the pace.

As we have noted, neoliberalism's principal target in the UK has been the reformist social-democratic welfare state. Though this was a radically compromised formation, which depended on dynamic capitalist growth to create the wealth for redistribution, its full-employment objectives, welfare support systems, the NHS, and free comprehensive and higher education, transformed the lives of millions. In this model the state took over some key services (water, bus transport, the railways), but it was less successful in nationalising productive industry (cars, energy, mining).

THE LIBERAL HERITAGE

Where do neoliberal ideas come from? Historically, they are rooted in the principles of 'classic' liberal economic and political theory. Here we can only outline the development of this body of ideas in summary, headline terms. Critical was the agrarian revolution, the expansion of markets (in land, labour, agriculture and commodities) and the rise of the first commercial-consumer society in eighteenth-century Britain. These arose on the back of successes in war, naval supremacy over continental rivals, the expansion of commerce, the conquest of India and a high point in the colonial slave plantation economies, which produced – often in conditions of un-free labour, violence and systematic degradation – commodities and profits for the metropolitan market: 'jewels in the crown', as the French called Saint-Domingue (Haiti) just before the Haitian Revolution.

Economically, its foundations lay in the rights of free men – 'masters of all they survey and captains of their souls' – to dispose of their property as they saw fit, to 'barter and truck', as Adam Smith put it, to make a profit and accumulate wealth, consulting only their own interests. Smith's *The Wealth of Nations* brilliantly 'codified' the economic model (using as an example no industrial enterprise larger than a pin factory!).

Marx once described this moment in the accumulation circuits of capital as 'the very Eden of the innate rights of man', the source of the lexicon of bourgeois ideas – freedom, equality, property and 'Bentham' (i.e. possessive individualism and self-interest):

> Freedom because both buyer and seller of a commodity … are constrained only by their own free-will. They contract as free agents … Equality because each enters into the relation with the other as with a simple owner of commodities and they exchange equivalent for equivalent. Property because each disposes of what is his own. And Bentham because each looks only to himself. The only force that brings them together and puts them in relation with each other is the selfishness, the gain and the private interests of each (*Capital*, 1, p112).

Political liberalism has its roots in the struggles of the rising classes associated with these developments to challenge, break and displace the tyranny of monarchical, aristocratic and landed power. Englishmen were born free: England was the true home of Liberty. This required the consent of free, propertied men to a limited form of state, and a leading position for them in society as well as wider political representation. Key moments were the Civil War; the execution of Charles 1; the 'historic compromise' of the 'Glorious Revolution' of 1688; the successes of the rising mercantile classes in commerce and trade; and the loss of the American colonies, but then in consolation a Lockean-inspired Constitution for an American Republic of free propertied men. Then came 1789, the violence and excessive egalitarianism of the

French Revolution, the successes of the Napoleonic Wars and the conservative reaction to civil unrest.

Industrialisation and the rise of manufacture followed in the nineteenth century: the 'disciplines' of waged labour, the factory system, the triumph of free trade, urbanisation and the industrial slum, as Britain became 'the workshop of the world'. Hobsbawm calls this triumph of the bourgeois classes, and of bourgeois ideas, modes of organisation, thought and value, 'The Age of Capital'. But radical currents that had awkwardly nestled beneath the commodious canopy of liberalism now began to chart another path: the Jacobin clubs, radicalism, the demonstrators of Peterloo, Chartism, the struggles over the franchise, cooperative and utopian communities, the early trade unions and friendly societies. This contradiction forced forward the 'age of reform' – struggles to extend the franchise; to impose limits on working hours, and on child and female labour; and for Catholic Emancipation, the abolition of slavery, repeal of the Combination Acts and the Corn Laws; but also propelled the gradual disengagement from Liberalism of an independent working-class interest.

Later, family businesses became consolidated into joint-stock companies – the basis of a corporate capitalist economy – which came to dominate domestic and imperial economic expansion. This development underpinned Britain as centre of the largest, most far-flung empire on earth, and facilitated the triumph of a liberal imperial class – 'the lords of creation' – and their 'civilising' mission.

These developments over two centuries form the core of classical liberal political and economic thought on which neoliberalism now dreams again. But here also begin the antinomies and ambiguities of liberalism. Political ideas of 'liberty' became harnessed to economic ideas of the free market: one of liberalism's intersecting fault-lines which re-emerges with neoliberalism. As Edmund Burke ironically observed: 'It would be odd to see the Guinea captain [of a slave ship] attempting at the same instant to publish his proclamation of Liberty and to advertise its sale of slaves'. But this is precisely the 'splitting' that Liberalism practised: Progress, but simultaneously the need to contain any 'threat from below'; tolerance, reform, moderation and representative government for the English race, but colonial governmentality, discipline and authority for recalcitrant 'other' native peoples abroad; emancipation *and* subjugation; free men in London, slaves in the West Indies; freedom now for some, an unending apprenticeship to freedom for others; the universal language of 'mankind' vs the particularity of the discourse of women; a civilising 'mission' that harboured an untranscended gulf between the civilised and the barbarians; today, the 'soft' face of compassionate conservatism and The Big Society here, the hard edge of cuts, workfare and the gospel of self-reliance there.

Classic liberal ideas began to decline in the late nineteenth century. Dangerfield cited the suffragettes, the trade unions, reform of the House of Lords (an old aristocratic bastion) and the struggle for Irish independence as key triggers of the 'Strange Death of Liberal England'. In an increasingly plutocratic society, there was a growing coalescence between land and capital: industrialists seeking respectability in their new country piles, while the old aristocratic and landed classes were pleased to travel to the City to invest, as the rate of profit from imperial trade soared. The new plutocratic classes took the world market as their oyster. But the sharpening competition with other states and the 'scramble' for imperial power led Lenin to describe imperialism as 'the highest stage of capitalism'.

Facing competition from Prussia and Japan, a New Liberalism emerged in Britain that embraced state intervention and 'the community' (as ever, a convenient half-way stop to class). The social insurance reforms of the Liberal Coalition of 1906-11 (Lloyd George and Churchill) laid down an early template for the welfare state. Later on, intervention against unemployment and the struggle against poverty – associated with Keynes and Beveridge – led the second phase. This is a history that Nick Clegg and the Lib Dems – grumpily clinging to the tail-coats of their Conservative Coalition allies – have conveniently forgotten or never understood.

The 1880s to the 1920s were a critical watershed that saw the rise of capitalist 'mass society': mass production, mass consumer markets, the market way of incorporating the masses into a subaltern position in the system, mass political parties and industrial unions, the mass media, mass culture, mass leisure, mass sport and entertainment, mass advertising, and new methods of marketing, testing and supplying the 'needs' of the masses and shaping demand – embryo forms of today's focus groups, life-style market segmentation, branding, personal relations consultancies, consumer services and the rest. The 'managerial revolution' – a new coalition of interests between share-holders and capital's senior managers – created not bourgeois entrepreneurs but the investor and executive classes of the giant multinational capitalist enterprises that now spanned the globe.

Neoliberalism, then, evolves. It borrows and appropriates extensively from classic liberal ideas; but each is given a further 'market' inflexion and conceptual revamp. Classic liberal principles have been radically transformed to make them applicable to a modern, global, post-industrial capitalism. In translating these ideas to different discursive forms and a different historical moment, neoliberalism performs a massive work of transcoding, while remaining in sight of the lexicon on which it draws. It is able do its dis-articulating and re-articulating work because these ideas have long been inscribed in social practices and institutions, and sedimented into the 'habitus' of everyday life, common sense and popular consciousness – 'traces without an inventory'.

Of course, transcoding can also be an opportunity for mystification. Thus Tory MP Jesse Norman, in *The Big Society*, quotes John Donne's wonderful affirmation of human inter-dependence: 'No man is an Island ... Any man's death diminishes me because I am involved in mankind'. Norman then goes on to quote De Tocqueville, as if he and Donne were saying the same thing: 'The more [the state] stands in the place of associations, the more will individuals, losing the notion of combining together, require its assistance'. This is a mischievous conflation, which the editorial addition of the '[the state]' has greatly helped on its way.

NEOLIBERALISM IN THE POSTWAR PERIOD: THATCHERISM AND BLAIRISM

How then has neoliberalism been nurtured, honed and developed across the post-war conjunctures? During the years that immediately followed the second world war there was a rare interlude – the 'Butler' moment – of near-consensus on the basic shape of the welfare state and mixed economy. But as the post-war economy revived, and the US replaced the UK as the 'paradigm instance', internal tensions came increasingly to the surface. Changes in the class structure and the spread of affluence provoked a crisis of confidence on the left. 'Can Labour survive the coming of the telly, the washing machine, the fridge and the small car?' Gaitskell asked anxiously. In the 1960s, rock music, the new youth culture, the decline of deference, the liberating effect for women of the contraceptive pill, the counterculture and mind-expanding drugs – all were straws in the wind of trouble to come: 'resistance through rituals'. '1968' unleashed an avalanche of protest, dissent and disaffiliation: student occupations, participatory democracy, community politics, second-wave feminism, 'turn on, tune in and drop out', an ambivalent libertarianism; but also the cult of 'Che' Guevara, Vietnam, the IRA, industrial unrest, black power, the red brigades ... While all this was going on, in the mid-1970s, and as inflation soared, the IMF, useful for imposing structural adjustment programmes on Third World states, imposed one on the British Chancellor. And in the dim light of the three-day week Ted Heath declared the country ungovernable. The post-war 'settlement' had collapsed.

In 1979 Thatcherism launched its assault on society and the Keynesian state. But simultaneously it began a fundamental recon-struction of the socio-economic architecture with the first privatisations. (One-nation Tory Harold Macmillan called it 'selling off the family silver'!) Thatcherism thoroughly confused the left. Could it be not just another swing of the electoral pendulum but the start of a reconstruc-tion of society along radically new, neoliberal lines?

Still, the old had to be destroyed before the new could take its place. Margaret Thatcher conspired in a ruthless war against the cabinet 'wets' and simultaneously plotted to break trade union power – 'the enemy within'. She impelled people towards new, individual-ised, competitive solutions: 'get on your bike', become self-employed or a share-holder, buy your council house, invest in the property-owning democracy. She coined a homespun equivalent for the key neoliberal ideas behind the sea-change she was imposing on society: value for money, managing your own budget, fiscal restraint, the money supply and the virtues of competition. There was anger, protest, resistance – but also a surge of populist support for the ruthless exer-cise of strong leadership.

Thatcherism mobilised widespread but unfocused anxiety about social change, engineering populist calls from 'below' to the state 'above' to save the country by imposing social order. This slide towards a 'law and order' society (see *Policing the Crisis*) was a key stage in the contradictory advance towards 'authoritarian populism'.[4]

One counter-intuitive feature was that, in the dark days of her electoral unpopularity, Thatcher brilliantly summoned to the rescue, not market rationality but an archaic British nationalism. The Falklands War allowed Thatcherism to play, when required, from two different ideological repertoires, with resonance in apparently opposing reservoirs of public sentiment: marching towards the future clad in the armour of the past. 'The market' was a modern, rational, efficient, practically-oriented discourse, inscribed in the everyday. Nationalist discourse, with its imperialist undertow (what Paul Gilroy calls its 'melancholia', the unrequited mourning for a lost object), was haunted by the fantasy of a late return to the flag, family values, national character, imperial glory and the spirit of Palmerstonian gunboat diplomacy.

Ideology is always contradictory. There is no single, integrated 'ruling ideology' – a mistake we repeat again now in failing to distinguish between conservative and neoliberal repertoires. Ideology works best by suturing together contradictory lines of argument and emotional investments – finding what Laclau called 'systems of equivalence' between them. Contradiction is its *metier*. Andrew Gamble characterised Thatcherism as combining 'free market'/'strong state'. Many believed this contradiction would be Thatcherism's undoing. But, though not logical, few strategies are so successful at winning consent as those which root themselves in the contradictory elements of common sense, popular life and consciousness. Even today, the market/free enterprise/private property discourse persists cheek by jowl with older conservative attachments to nation, racial homogeneity, Empire, tradition. 'Market forces' is good for restoring the power of capital and destroying the redistributivist illusion. But in moments of difficulty one can trust 'the Empire' to strike back. 'The people' will turn out to cheer the fleet returning to Plymouth from some South Atlantic speck of land; they will line the streets of Wootton Bassett to honour the returning dead from 'a war without end' in Afghanistan. (How many remembered this was Britain's *fourth* Afghan War?)

In the end Thatcherism was too socially destructive and ideologically extreme to triumph in its 'scorched earth' form. Even her cabinet fan-club knew it could not last. But it was a 'conviction moment' they will never forget. And today, once again, many yearn to return to it in some more consolidated, permanent and settled form.

Paradoxically, such a form was provided by Blair's hybrid, New Labour, which abandoned Labour's historic agenda and set about reconstructing social democracy as 'the best shell' for a New Labour variant of neoliberalism. Hybrid, because – borrowing the skills of triangulation (one idea from each end of the political spectrum to make a 'Third Way') from Clinton – it re-articulated social reform, free enterprise and the market. This conflation was the real source of New Labour 'spin' – not an irritating habit but a serious political strategy, a 'double shuffle'. New Labour repositioned itself from centre-left to centre-right. Covered by that weasel word, 'modernisation', the New Labour 'saints' remorselessly savaged 'Old' Labour. A substantial sector of Labour's 'heartland' left, never to return. But the 'middle ground', the pin-head on which all mainstream parties now compete to dance, became the privileged political destination.

New Labour believed that the old route to government was permanently barred. It was converted, Damascus-like, to neoliberalism and the market. And, buying in to the new managerial doctrine of pubic choice theory taught by the US Business Schools, New Labour finally understood that there was no need for the political hassle to privatise. You could simply burrow underneath the distinction between state and market. Out-sourcing, value-for-money and contract-contestability criteria opened one door after another through which private capital could slip into the public sector and hollow it out from within. This meant New Labour adopting market strategies, submitting to competitive disciplines, espousing entrepreneurial values and constructing new entrepreneurial subjects. Tony Giddens, a Third Way pioneer, is supposed to have told Blair that nothing could resist 'the unstoppable advance of market forces'. 'Marketisation' became the cutting-edge of New Labour's neoliberal project.

New Labour thus embraced 'managerial marketisation'. The economy was actively 'liberalised' (with disastrous consequence for the coming crisis), while society was boxed in by legislation, regulation, monitoring, surveillance and the ambiguous 'target' and 'control' cultures. It adopted 'light-touch' regulation. But its 'regulators' lacked teeth, political courage, leverage or an alternative social philosophy, and were often playing on both sides of the street. Harnessing social purposes to a free-wheeling private economy proved to be an exercise much like Tawney's 'trying to skin a tiger stripe by stripe'.

There were social problems requiring urgent attention, but what was most striking was New Labour's moralistically driven legislative zeal in its approach to them: ASBOs, community policing, widening surveillance, private policing and security firms, out-sourcing the round-up and expulsion of visa-less migrants, imprisonment of terrorist suspects without trial, and ultimately complicity with rendition and a 'cover-up' of involvement with torture. Despite the 'liberalism', punitive conceptions of punishment took hold: longer sentences, tougher prison regimes, harsher youth-offender disciplines. A new kind of liberal 'authoritarianism' turned out to be one of the jokers in New Labour's neoliberal pack. Michael Howard declared that 'prison works', implying that those who thought it didn't were 'bleeding-heart liberals'. Blair, certainly not one, espoused 'tough love'. (Later David Cameron invented 'muscular liberalism'!) This is certainly not the first time these two contradictory Janus-faces of Liberalism have been evident.

New Labour did initiate very important social reforms, including the minimum wage, shorter waiting times, better health targets, attempts to reduce child poverty, the doubling of student numbers and (rather reluctantly) some equality and human rights legislation. But triangulation was its life-blood, its leading tendency. There was a continuous tension between a strident, Fabian, Benthamite tendency to regulate and manage and the ideology of the market, with its pressure for market access to areas of public life from which it had hitherto been excluded. Regulation was often the site of a struggle to resolve the contradiction between an enhanced role for the private sector and the need to demonstrate positive outcomes. But there was a strong impulse towards getting rid of the excrescences of the 'nanny state', in areas such as planning and health and safety regulations, and towards 'flexibility' in labour markets.

What was distinctively neoliberal about New Labour's strategies? The private funding of New Labour's flagship achievements via the Public Finance Initiative left future generations in hock for thirty years to re-pay the debt at exorbitant interest rates. Yet 'public-private partnership' became a required condition of all public contracts. Contracting out, competitive tendering and 'contestability' opened up the state to capital. Private contractors were better placed to cut costs and shed staff, even at the expense of service quality. The rising archipelago of private companies providing public services for profit was spectacular. Consultants floated in and out to 'educate' the public sphere in the ways of corporate business. Senior public servants joined the Boards of their private suppliers through 'the revolving door'.

Emptied out from inside, the ethos of public service underwent an irreversible 'culture change'. The habits and assumptions of the private sector became embedded in the state.

Neoliberal discourse promoted two discursive figures – the 'taxpayer' (hard-working man, over-taxed to fund the welfare 'scrounger') and the 'customer' (fortunate housewife, 'free' to exercise limited choice in the market-place, for whom the 'choice agenda' and personalised delivery were specifically designed). No-one ever thinks either could also be a citizen who needs or relies on public services.

The prevailing market discourse is, of course, a matter of ideological representation – a point that Doreen Massey develops in Chapter 7. Actual markets do not work that way. They do not work mysteriously by themselves, or 'clear' at their optimum point. Only by bracketing-out the relative wealth of buyer and seller can they be called 'fair'. No 'hidden hand' guarantees the common good. Markets often require the external power of state and law to establish and regulate them. But the discourse provides subjects with a 'lived' 'imaginary relation' to their real conditions of existence. This does not mean that markets are simply manufactured fictions. Indeed, they are only too real! They are 'false' because they offer partial explanations as an account of whole processes. But it is worth remembering that 'those things which we believe to be true are "real" in their consequences'.

Globally, New Labour agreed that 'developing countries' must be exposed to the bracing winds of Free Trade and foreign investment. The main purpose of global governance was to protect markets and investments and maintain the conditions for the successful pursuit of global capitalist enterprise. This required a major commitment to a new geopolitical order, military expenditure, and the construction of a ring of client states and dictators, many of whom routinely used repression, violence, imprisonment and torture; and, if necessary, direct military intervention – though naturally in humanitarian disguise.

The Blair experiment ended unexpectedly – the result of long subservience to US foreign policy goals. The 'special relationship' guaranteed the UK a role as geopolitical junior partner and a place in the global sun. It stood 'shoulder to shoulder' against the rise of Islamic fundamentalism. George Bush, supported by the neoconservative lobby, led Blair into armed intervention and regime change in Iraq. Blair's moralism was compromised by his specious logic, dissembling, secret agreements of which everyone was kept in ignorance, sexed-up documents and flawed intelligence. His reputation has never recovered.

Gordon Brown, who followed, did not fundamentally alter New Labour's neoliberal inclinations. Never a paid-up 'Third Way' proselytiser, his manse background, high moral seriousness and early Labour formation stood in the way. The positive side of New Labour's 'double shuffle' became identified with him: public investment, limiting third-world debt and child poverty. But 'redistribution by stealth' failed to build a political constituency or a principled defence of the welfare state.

Besides, Brown admired the dynamism of American free-enterprise capitalism. He fell for the profoundly mistaken belief that Labour had somehow ended the cycle of 'boom and bust'. He did not heed the signs that the boom could not last forever – the uncontrollable property market, the swelling private and public debt, the dubious risk-taking devices invented by ambitious young traders, the unregulated predations of the hedge-fund and private equity sectors, the scandal of banks selling sub-prime mortgages worth more than many borrowers' total annual income, the enhancement of share values, the astronomic executive salaries and bonuses, banking's shift to risk-taking investment activities. These were all signs a sophisticated economic technician like Brown should not have missed. In the crisis Brown's international leadership was impressive, but it was all too late. Neoliberal hubris had done its damage. By the time of the election (which Brown should have called a year before), it was clear Labour would lose. It did.

THE COALITION VARIANT

A Conservative-Liberal Democratic coalition was fully in line with the dominant political logic of realignment. In the spirit of the times, Cameron, with Blair as his role model, signalled his determination to reposition the Tories as a 'compassionate conservative party', though this has turned out to be a something of a chimera.

At the same time, many underestimated how deeply being out of office and power had divided the Lib-Dem soul, and misjudged the self-deception, hypocrisy and lack of principle of which the Lib-Dem leadership was capable. Coalition now set the neoliberal-inclined *Orange Book* supporters, who favoured an alliance with the

Conservatives, against the 'progressives', including former social democrats, who leaned towards Labour. A deal – its detail now forgotten – was stitched up, in which the social liberals were trounced, and Cameron and Clegg 'kissed hands' in the No. 10 rose garden (the former looking like the cat that had swallowed the cream). The Lib Dems thus provided the Cameron leadership with the 'fig leaf' it needed – while the banking crisis gave the 'alibi'. The Coalition government seized the opportunity to launch the most radical, far-reaching and irreversible social revolution since the war.

Coalition policy often seems incompetent, with failures to think things through or join things up. But, from another angle, it is arguably the best prepared, most wide-ranging, radical and ambitious of the three regimes which since the 1970s have been maturing the neoliberal project. The Conservatives had for some time been devoting themselves to preparing for office – not in policy detail but in terms of how policy could be used in power to legislate into effect a new political 'settlement'. They had convinced themselves that deep, fast cuts would have to be made to satisfy the bond markets and international assessors. But could the crisis be used, as Friedman had suggested, to 'produce real change'?

The legislative avalanche began immediately and has not let up. It begins negatively ('the mess the previous government left us') but ends positively, in embracing radical structural reform as the solution. Ideology is in the driving seat, though vigorously denied. The front-bench ideologues – Osborne, Lansley, Gove, Maude, Duncan Smith, Pickles, Hunt – are saturated in neoliberal ideas and determined to give them legislative effect. As *One Flew over the Cuckoo's Nest* put it, 'The crazies are in charge of the asylum'. They are single-minded about the irreversible transformation of society, ruthless about the means, and in denial about the 'fall-out'. Osborne – smirking, clever, cynical, 'the smiler with the knife' – wields the chopper with zeal. Cameron – relaxed, plausible, charming, confident, a silver-spooned patrician, 'a smooth man' – 'fronts' the Coalition TV show. This crew long ago accepted Schumpeter's adage that there is no alternative to 'creative destruction'. They have given themselves, through legislative manoeuvring, an uninterrupted five years to accomplish this task.

Its wide-ranging character must be judged in terms of the operational breadth of the institutions and practices they aim to 'reform', their boldness in siphoning state-funding to the private sector, and the number of constituencies they are prepared to confront. Reform and choice – words already hijacked by New Labour – are the master narrative. They may be Conservatives but this is *not* a 'conserving' regime (it is a bemused Labour which is toying with the 'blue-Labour' conservative alternative now). Tories and Lib Dems monotonously repeat the dissembling mantras of their press and public relations people: 'we are clearing up the mess inherited from the previous government'. But the neoliberal engine is at full throttle.

We cannot deal with the cuts in any detail here. They have only just started and there is much more to come. Instead we limit ourselves to tracking the neoliberal logic behind the strategy.

First, targeted constituencies – i.e. anyone associated with, relying or dependent on the state and public services. For the rich, the recession never happened. For the public sector, however, there will be massive redundancies, a wage freeze, pay running well behind the rate of inflation, pensions which will not survive in their present form, rising retirement ages. Support for the less well off and the vulnerable will be whittled away, and welfare dependency broken. Benefits will be capped, workfare will be enforced. The old must sell homes to pay for care; working parents must buy child care; and invalidity benefit recipients must find work. Sure Start, the schools refurbishment programme and Independent Maintenance Grants are on hold. Wealthy parents can buy children an Oxbridge education, but many other students will go into life-long debt to get a degree. You cannot make £20 billion savings in the NHS without affecting front-line, clinical and nursing services. Andrew Lansley, however, 'does not recognise that figure'. Similarly, though everybody else knew most universities would charge the maximum £9000 tuition fees, David 'Two-Brain' Willetts doesn't recognise that figure. Saying that square pegs fit into round holes has become a front-bench speciality.

Women stand where many of these savage lines intersect. As Beatrix Campbell reminds us, cutting the state means minimising the arena in which women can find a voice, allies, social as well as material support; and in which their concerns can be recognised. It means reducing the resources society collectively allocates to children, to making children a shared responsibility, and to the general 'labour' of care and love.

Second, there is privatisation – returning public and state services to private capital, re-drawing the social architecture. Privatisation comes in three sizes: (1) straight sell-off of public assets; (2) contracting out to private companies for profit; (3) two-step privatisation 'by stealth', where it is represented as an unintended consequence. Some examples: in criminal justice, contracts for running prisons are being auctioned off, and in true neoliberal fashion Ken Clarke says he cannot see any difference in principle whether prisons are publicly or privately owned; in health care, the private sector is already a massive, profit-making presence, having cherry-picked for profit medical services that hospitals can no longer afford to provide; while in the most far-reaching, top-down NHS reorganisation, GPs and other professionals, grouped into private consortia, will take charge of the £60 billion health budget. Since few GPs know how or have time to run complex budgets, they will 'naturally' turn to the private health companies, who are circling the NHS like sharks waiting to feed. Primary Care Trusts, which represented a public interest in the funding process, are being scrapped. In the general spirit of 'competition', hospitals must remove the 'cap' on the number of private patients they treat.

Third, the lure of 'localism'. In line with David Cameron's Big Society, 'free schools' (funded from the public purse – Gove's revenge) will 'empower' parents and devolve power to 'the people'. But parents – beset as they are by pressing domestic and care responsibilities, and lacking the capacity to run schools, assess good teaching, define balanced curricula, remember much science or the new maths, or speak a foreign language, while regarding history as boring, and not having read a serious novel since GCSE – will have to turn to the private education sector to manage schools and define the school's 'vision'. Could the two-step logic be clearer?

Fourth, phoney populism: pitching 'communities' against local democracy. Eric Pickles intends to wean councils permanently off the central grant system. Meanwhile, social housing is at a standstill, housing benefits will be cut and council rents allowed to rise to commercial levels in urban centres. Many will move to cheaper rentals, losing networks of friends, child support, family, school friends and school places. Parents must find alternative employment locally – if there is any – or allow extra travelling time. Jobseekers' allowances will be capped. As the private housing lobby spokesperson said, 'we are looking forward to a bonanza'. Since the early days of Thatcher we have not seen such a ferocious onslaught on the fabric of civil society, relationships and social life.

Fifth, cutting down to size state involvement in quality of life. Amenities like libraries, parks, swimming baths, sports facilities, youth clubs, community centres will either be privatised or disappear. Either unpaid volunteers will 'step up to the plate' or doors will close. In truth, the aim is not – in the jargon of '1968' from which the promiscuous Cameron is not ashamed to borrow – to 'shift power to the people', but to undermine the structures of local democracy. The left, which feels positively about volunteering, community involvement and participation – and who doesn't? – finds itself once again triangulated into uncertainty. The concept of the 'Big Society' is so empty that universities have been obliged to put it at the top of their research agenda on pain of a cut in funding – presumably so that politicians can discover what on earth it means: a shabby, cavalier, duplicitous interference in freedom of thought.

What is intended is a permanent revolution. Can society be permanently reconstructed along these lines? Is neoliberalism hegemonic?

The protests are growing. Weighty professional voices are ranged against structural reforms, and the speed and scale of cuts in a fragile economy. There are pauses, rethinks and u-turns. There may be more. If the Lib-Dem 'wheeze' of delivering cuts in government and campaigning against them at the next election fails to persuade, they face the prospect of an electoral wipe-out. The Coalition may fall apart, though at an election the Conservatives might get the majority they failed to muster last time. What happens next is not pregiven.

Hegemony is a tricky concept and provokes muddled thinking. No project achieves 'hegemony' as a completed project. It is a process, not a state of being. No victories are permanent or final. Hegemony has constantly to be 'worked on', maintained, renewed, revised. Excluded social forces, whose consent has not been won, whose interests have not been taken into account, form the basis of counter-movements, resistance, alternative strategies and visions … and the struggle over a hegemonic system starts anew. They constitute what Raymond Williams called 'the emergent' – and are the reason why history is never closed but maintains an open horizon towards the future.

However, in ambition, depth, degree of break with the past, variety of sites being colonised, impact on common sense and shift in the social architecture, neoliberalism does constitute a *hegemonic project*, a theme that Doreen Massey takes up in Chapter 5. Today, popular thinking and the systems of calculation in daily life offer very little friction to the passage of its ideas. Delivery may be more difficult: new and old contradictions still haunt the edifice, in the very process of its reconstruction. Still, in terms of laying foundations and staging the future on favourable ground, the neoliberal project is several stages further on. To traduce a phrase of Marx's: 'well grubbed, old mole'. Alas!

NOTES

1. David Harvey, *A Brief History of Neoliberalism*, OUP 2007.
2. Nik Theodore, Jamie Peck and Neil Brenner, 'Neoliberal Urbanism: Cities and the Rule of Markets', in Sophie Watson and Gary Bridge (eds), *The New Blackwell Companion to the City*, Wiley 2011, p15.
3. Friedrich Hayek, Preface, 1982 edition *Capitalism and Freedom*, first published 1962.
4. S. Hall, C Critcher, J. Jefferson, J. Clarke and B. Roberts, *Policing the Crisis*, Macmillan 1978.

2. REFLECTIONS ON THE PRESENT

Michael Rustin

This chapter analyses the implications of the credit crunch – that is to say the severe crisis which has been afflicting the global economy for the past two years or so – through conceiving of these events as a 'conjuncture'. This is a theoretical term that refers to a critical turning-point or rupture in a political structure, primarily signifying a crisis in class relations. Classically, in Marxist and especially Leninist political discourse, these have been moments in which forceful political leaders – such as Robespierre, Lenin or Mao – have been able to seize hold of exceptional political moments. Such occasions of tension and disequilibrium have of course provided opportunities for counter-revolutionaries of the right – Mussolini and fascism, Hitler and national socialism – as well as for movements of the left. The concept of conjuncture had its most effective application, within the 'new left' tradition to which *Soundings* belongs, in analysing the crisis of the 1970s, which as everyone knows ushered in the thirty years or so of neoliberal hegemony which now may (or may not) be coming to its end.[1]

The concept of conjuncture was developed in the middle years of the last century as a way of thinking through the manifest misalignment with political realities of classical deterministic and economistic Marxist models of change. Contrary to classical predictions, western capitalism appeared, from the late 1950s, to be producing a rise rather than a fall in the living standards of the working class, and the working class was becoming more socially and politically divided rather than growing into a homogeneous and radical social force. Two fields of neo-Marxist theory contributed most to understanding the emerging situation.

On the one hand there were Antonio Gramsci's ideas, which contributed an understanding of the complexity of regimes of class domination and subordination, and of the importance of the cultural dimensions of the social order in maintaining these. Further, Gramsci had theorised the necessity to adopt political strategies appropriate to a particular social configuration, as in his distinction between a 'war of manoeuvre' (of which Leninism was the classic proponent), and a 'war of position' – which he deemed the more appropriate political strategy within the more consensual civil societies of western Europe. Thus autonomous political action, undertaken in response to analysis of a particular societal configuration, was given a new emphasis within Marxist thought.

Complementary to the engagement with Gramsci's ideas was the influence of Louis Althusser. He also challenged classical notions of economic determinism, by proposing a complex and multi-levelled model of the social order, in which, as with Gramsci, the 'levels' of ideology and the organisation of the state exercised their own causal powers. The classical Marxist idea of determination through the agency of the means and relations of production was 'saved', in Althusser's account, by his assertion that this level of domination would prevail only 'in the last instance' – by which he seemed to be referring not to a final day of decisive political judgement but to a model of causal powers in which the economy ruled (if it did) only as the most weighty of a whole assembly of forces.[2] The complex inter-relations of 'levels and instances' of the social formation were held to be such that models of linear causal determination (such as that implied in the classical model of 'base and superstructure') did not work. The new explanatory model, rather, presupposed an ever-shifting interrelationship between contending and interdependent social forces. This complexity was characterised by instances of 'over-determination' (and logically, therefore, under-determination too), in which causal forces could converge on a particular, often contingent, point of weakness or imbalance, and an opportunity for rupture thereby occur.[3]

This way of modelling social processes borrowed some of its conceptions of causal interdependency from the then-dominant sociological functionalism of Talcott Parsons et al, except that Althusser's primary purpose was to understand the possible occurrence of points of break-down, whereas the functionalists sought to theorise the many reasons why patterns of social life might be expected to reproduce themselves in a stable mode. Furthermore, what was seen by the functionalists as a dominant, structurally necessary and virtuous value-system was conceived by Althusser as ideology – a distinct level of the social order whose main function was to maintain and legitimise class domination. To ideology Althusser counterposed a materialist, scientific mode of reasoning, through which underlying social relations could be understood, and perhaps surpassed.[4]

We can now see similarities between the theoretical model of complex interdependencies that Althusser evolved to enable Marxist analysis to cope with the emerging world of late capitalism, and the subsequent development by mathematicians, computer scientists, biologists and general systems theorists of what is known as 'complexity theory'.[5] This way of thinking, or paradigm, was evolved to make it possible to understand complex systems in the physical, biological and social realms that were characterised by non-linear patterns of causation, disequilibria and drastic changes of state, and emergent properties. Kingsley Dennis and John Urry have recently sought to apply this methodology to understand what they see as the impending end of a socio-technical system based on the automobile and the consumption of oil, and its large potential consequences for global society.[6] The 'tipping points' of complexity theory can be understood as the equivalent of 'conjunctures' – those moments, according to late Marxist theory, in which decisive transformations can occur. One might think of speculative bubbles as such complex systems.

A crucial context for the emergence of these new models of explanation lay in the events of May 1968, in which what seemed like a moment of proto-revolutionary upheaval emerged in Paris 'from nowhere' – being first triggered off by grievances that seemed to have little to do with the economy (the threatened closing of the Cinemateque, police brutality, conditions in the university) – and seemed primarily to engage university and high school students before the uprising became extended to the factories and the organised working class. However, the exemplary deployment of this 'method' of analysis took place not in relation to that radical moment of transformation in which the left was the principal agent, but, as we have noted, in analysis of the developments in the late 1970s that led to the triumph of Reagan in the United States, Thatcher in Britain, and then to the thirty-year (and continuing) hegemony of what is widely called 'neoliberalism'.

In *Policing the Crisis: Mugging, the State and Law and Order* (see note 1), Stuart Hall et al followed a thread first picked up in the response of the press in Birmingham to an alleged wave of 'mugging' (roughly defined as black-on-white street crime), which became a major moral panic in the mass media. The authors described the mobilisation of white anxieties about race as a key ingredient in the emergence of a new politics of the right, exploited by Nixon in the United States and by Thatcher, following Enoch Powell's example, in Britain. Presciently, they anticipated the possibility of a reconfiguration of working-class political loyalties away from the solidarities of class. They saw this being achieved in the context of the much broader state of delegitimation and disorder that had come to prevail throughout the 1970s. Hall and his colleagues here theorised the protracted crisis and failure of the entire 'class settlement' of the post-war welfare state. Successive governments of both hues had proved themselves unable to cope with the increasing levels of social tension that had found expression in rising levels of inflation and industrial conflict. Indeed three successive governments (Wilson in 1970, Heath in 1974 and Callaghan in 1979) had been defeated, in effect, by trade union resistance to governments' demands for wage restraint. *Policing the Crisis* described the long moment of 'corporatism', in which 'consensual' and 'centrist' resolutions of this fundamental disequilibrium of class relations were attempted, with increasing desperation, until public confidence in these approaches finally failed amidst the events of the 'Winter of Discontent' of 1978-79. The extremity of this 'conjuncture' was due in part to 'external' factors, such as the soaring price of oil, which was itself a lagged inflationary effect of the Vietnam War. But conjunctural analysis presupposes, by definition, elements of contingency and 'overdetermination', of which in this period there were many.

This was a moment in which it became possible to reconfigure political forces, and, in an unusually open situation, to construct by decisive action what turned out to become a lasting neoliberal hegemony. In *Policing the Crisis*, and in his subsequent seminal articles in *Marxism Today* and *Soundings*, on Thatcherism and its New Labour sequel, Stuart Hall clarified the significance of the ideological and political dimensions of the new right's successful project, leaving much of the analysis of the more economic and technological dimensions of this neoconservative reshaping of the world to other writers, in *Marxism Today* and elsewhere.

THE PRESENT CRISIS

How might this method of analysis be relevant to an understanding of the present crisis? What are the similarities, and differences, between the events which led to the triumph of neoliberalism from the late 1970s until recently, and events between 2007 and 2009 that have now administered at the very least a major setback to this system?

The most significant difference between these two episodes is that the earlier one was the outcome of a decade or more of severe and prolonged conflicts between different groups of collective actors within capitalism, whereas the current crisis has emerged in the absence of major social conflicts of this kind. In the former crisis, a neoconservative counter-revolution sought to rescue capitalism from its presumed enemies; in the present conjuncture a neoliberal system of domination seems to have imploded not long after it achieved its greatest moment of triumph over its ideological enemies, the collapse of European Communism in 1989. How can one compare and analyse moments of structural breakdown of such apparently different kinds?

It is interesting to observe the key conceptual role of money in these crisis situations. In the 1930s Keynes advocated the injection of money into the economy as a remedy for the Great Depression. Then, following the doctrine of Milton Friedman, the Thatcherites argued that an excess of money was responsible for the inflationary pressures of the 1970s, with their various consequences of rising claims and demands of all kinds. They therefore deployed monetary contraction in the 1980s as an instrument of deliberate recession and de-industrialisation: the ideological construction of the money-supply as an inflationary engine was a means of redressing what had come to be seen by the right as a threatening balance of class forces. However, once this deflationary purpose had been accomplished, faith in the possibility or desirability of controlling the supply of money was abandoned. The supply of money was belatedly discovered to be hard even to define, let alone control. Indeed, once the battle against inflation had been won, the money-supply was allowed to expand exponentially through the creation of vast amounts of credit, both on a local and a global scale. And so long as this expansion of credit (virtual money) seemed to be leading to general profit, few objected to it. The issue about money turned out to have been not whether there was too much or too little of it, but rather into whose pockets it was flowing.

Perhaps one could suggest that what mainly differentiates these different crises are the underlying structures of class relations of which they are an effect: different kinds of class equilibrium, or disequilibrium, have generated their typical forms of 'excess'. High levels of wage inflation, such as were seen in the 1970s, are a symptom of the pressure on profit levels of working-class demands, in conditions of full employment or scarce labour supply. Speculative manias, by contrast, are the excesses brought about by the unfettered power of the propertied. The motivations of individual self-interest that are fundamental to capitalism become transmuted into delusions about the unlimited prospects for gain (what the former Chair of the Federal Reserve Alan Greenspan called 'irrational exuberance'), as the reality constraints sometimes imposed by markets melt away (for example the need to reach negotiated accommodations with labour if steady production is to take place). The main reality that is denied by the powerful in these excesses is the significance of other social actors, and the larger totality of social relations on which all economies depend.

At this point it will be useful to make use of another valuable theoretical resource, the contrast between 'system' and 'social' integration' set out by David Lockwood in his seminal paper on this theme.[8] This was an attempt to develop functionalist sociological theory to take account of the prevalence of deep-seated class conflicts within European social structures, and to incorporate into functionalist discourse ideas of contradictions and class consciousness drawn from Marxist theory. Lockwood developed these ideas in the context of the rise of class tensions in the 1960s, when he and John Goldthorpe developed their distinction between instrumental and expressive solidarity, which proved invaluable in understanding the evolution of working-class consciousness in an 'economistic' direction in that period. It also did much to explain the later susceptibility of skilled working-class voters to Thatcher's advocacy of free wage bargaining in the late 1970s, in opposition to the Wilson-Callaghan governments' clumsy attempts to impose incomes policies, justified in part on egalitarian and solidaristic grounds.

Lockwood differentiated between states of disequilibrium in the social order that were the outcome of 'objectively' incompatible forces, and states of disequilibrium that resulted from conflicts between groups of social actors pursuing incompatible goals. In the crisis of the 1970s, social conflicts between class and other, emergent, collectivities and cultures (those of gender, race, generation, religious and, in Northern Ireland, nationalist identification) generated high levels of political tension, even leading to the belief in the political establishment – and elsewhere – that Britain was becoming 'ungovernable', in consequence of heightened social demands that the governmental system was unable to meet.[9] These contradictions were both 'social' and 'systemic' in their nature and effects. Heightened working-class demands in conditions of prolonged full employment, and rising levels of welfare expenditure resulting from political demands for 'social guarantees', gave rise to falling levels of profit and to a changing balance between state and private expenditure.[10] These were highly unwelcome to the interests of capital, as the verdicts on the British economy by international agencies such as the IMF and OECD made clear. It was thus the conjunction of both 'system' and 'social' contradictions that led to the crisis of the post-war welfare settlement, and to the 'counter-revolutionary' project of the new right, which found and then made its opportunity in this crisis.

In contrast to all this, the present crisis has plainly not been brought about by manifest social conflicts of a class-based or any other kind. If the neoliberal system has now encountered a crisis in its growth and development, it is not because it has been shaken by the opposition or resistance of the social forces it set out to defeat. Indeed, as contributors to *Soundings* have frequently pointed out, one of the greatest successes of the neoconservative counter-revolution has been the demobilisation of class resistances to capital, and the successful co-option of the political parties originally set up to represent working-class interests to the task of co-managing the marketised social and economic model. Not only was the financial meltdown *not* preceded by political or economic demands from below, but no sense of heightened political consciousness has so far emerged in response to the crisis itself. The dominant political mood, in Britain at least, is one of widespread disenchantment with the system of governance in its entirety.

Thus what we are seeing is not so much the *explosion* of conflicting social forces, as the *implosion* of a largely unchallenged political and economic system. In this respect, as many observers have pointed out, the nearest parallel to the present crisis is the crash of 1929 and the following depression. Indeed, one of the best ways of understanding what has been happening between 2007 and 2009 is to read about the 1929 events in J.K. Galbraith's *The Great Crash*. Galbraith's description of the operations of the banks and other financial agencies at that time, and of the rise and fall of speculative 'bubbles', shows extraordinary similarities between the events of that period and the patterns we have seen unfolding in the last year or two.

But if the present crisis is not the outcome of conflicts between politically conscious collective actors, what *are* its causes? What analysis will enable us to understand the 'system contradictions' that have brought us to this situation, and what, if any, political conclusions can we draw from this?

SYSTEMIC CONTRADICTIONS IN THE MARKETISED SYSTEM

Central to debate about the current crisis is, of course, the role of the financial and banking sectors. This is unsurprising, since it was the collapse of banks such as Lehman Brothers in the USA, and RBS and Lloyds in the UK, and of mortgage lenders such as Fannie Mae and Freddy Mac in the USA and Northern Rock and the Bradford and Bingley in the UK, which triggered the crisis. These collapses were brought about by the weight of bad debts that were accumulated in a vast wave of speculative investment. The insolvency of the banks has led to a general liquidity crisis, and the withdrawal of borrowing facilities from both businesses and individuals; and the outcome of this situation has been a substantial downturn in economic activity. The risk is that, as companies lay off workers to protect their profit-levels (and perhaps to avoid bankruptcy), consumer demand will fall further, and more redundancies follow, in a classic deflationary cycle.

An important difference between the present crisis and that of 1929 is that most governments have understood much sooner, and better, than their predecessors the need for concerted remedial actions by the state. Gordon Brown has been to the fore in international efforts to stave off a deep recession through counter-cyclical measures (cutting interest rates, programmes of public investment, 'printing money'); and these measures offer some prospect that the current recession will be less catastrophic than that of the 1930s. He has won support for his efforts from contemporary successors of Galbraith, such as Paul Krugman. The conventional wisdom appears to be that the structural causes of this crisis lie principally in the excesses of the financial sector, and that if the banks and other financial agencies can be subject to greater restraint and regulation it should be possible before long to return to 'business as usual', with only minor adjustments to the way global and national economies function.

However, there seems good reason to believe that this analysis of the problem is superficial, indeed false. The financial system is not merely a rogue element in an otherwise well-functioning economic system, and its near-meltdown was not a merely contingent event. The reality is that the malfunctioning of the financial sector in late capitalism is a symptom as much as a cause of the current crisis. The 'system contradictions' at the core of the matter are those which explain *why* the financial sector has become so hyper-inflated, in relation to the rest of the productive economy. These are issues of structure, not of mere irresponsible performance, and only if these can be addressed is there any hope of a lasting solution to the current problems.

John Bellamy Foster and Fred Magdoff have provided the most insightful analysis of the fundamental problem.[11] They argue that the hyper-expansion of the financial sector, especially in the United States, is the consequence of the decline of profitable opportunities for the investment of capital, other than financial speculation, since the 1980s. The over-development of the financial system is thus the effect, more than the cause, of the primary economic problem. Investors have engaged in parasitic speculative financial investment because there have been no better profitable opportunities; in the US financial profits have been growing as a proportion of gross profits since 1985. And the reason for the decline in opportunities for profitable investment is the stagnation, or decline, over a twenty-year period, in the real incomes of the majority of people with average or lower incomes. The consequence of declining real incomes among the worse-off was vividly manifested in the role of 'sub-prime loans' in triggering the financial crisis, but it is of more general provenance than this.[12]

To understand how this situation has come about we need to go back to the neoconservative resolution of the inflationary crisis of the 1970s. It was a deliberate purpose of the neoliberal offensive to shift income and power away from labour and towards property and capital, and to diminish the role of the state as an agent of redistribution and social justice. The deregulation of capital flows was designed to create a globalised market, and to expose the allegedly over-protected labour forces of the 'advanced' economies to competition from lower-wage economies. (The policies of the European Single Market pursue these objectives on a more restricted regional basis, its redistributive social programmes having a minor countervailing role.) Technology, especially information technology, which permits vast instant flows of money, also played a role in this globalising process, as well as the declining relative costs of transport. Far from being an embarrassment to the holders of power in this neoliberal system, inequality was actually celebrated, most notoriously in Britain in Peter Mandelson's 'we are intensely relaxed about people getting filthy rich'. A relative decline in average consumption was thus a concomitant of the marketisation and globalisation of the economy. But the inequalities that the neoliberals and globalisers sought as an object of policy have now become a major source of dysfunction and implosion for the entire market system.[13] The chosen resolution of the social conflicts and contradictions that underlay the earlier crisis has now been revealed as a primary source of the systemic contradictions that underlie the current conjuncture. Although different in their form, these two crises *are*, after all, connected.

There is also a major global aspect to this situation. One might have expected that enhanced purchasing power in the emerging economies of the south and east, which were (sometimes) beneficiaries of globalisation in terms of the financial flows and investments of globalisation, would offset the stagnation of incomes in the affluent north and west. But this counter-cyclical expansion in demand is yet to occur. This is because the emerging economies owe much of their competitive advantage to their low wages and severe labour discipline. They are for the most part in a different phase of development from that in the affluent west, still giving their priority to savings, capital accumulation and investment, where the west has long since been immersed in its devotion to mass consumption. A consequence of this juxtaposition of contrasting but interdependent economic worlds is the bizarre situation whereby China has become the major funder of the large American current accounts deficit (and thus its continuing high levels of consumption) through its loans to the USA of the vast surpluses earned by its exports.

This unexpected symbiosis between the over-consuming United States and the under-consuming People's Republic of China seemed to work for a period, in a time of economic growth, but it seems highly unlikely that expanded borrowings from China will now serve as the engine to lift the economies of the west out of their recession. It is widely recognised that China must now turn its attention to the expansion of domestic demand. A recent *Financial Times* article argued that a public commitment by China to the creation of a universal system of public health would make a crucial contribution to global economic recovery.[14] This is because it is only when a welfare 'safety net' exists that citizens feel secure enough to expand their consumption at the expense of savings. What a remarkable coincidence it is that both China and the United States are currently seeking a solution to problems of underconsumption (among other purposes) in major reforms of their health systems!

That the 'system contradictions' have been near-catastrophic in their effects, while there has been a much weaker presence of overt 'social contradictions', suggests that we might think of the impoverished – both in the United States and elsewhere in the world – as constituting a kind of 'shadow class', a passive but nevertheless significant factor in the situation. This 'shadow class' (or, as Marxists used to say, a class 'in itself but not for itself') has featured as the prime constituent of the 'sub-prime' mortage market, and also as the large segment (47 million) of the US population who cannot afford health insurance: a post-industrial economy also has its large working class, however it may perceive itself. In China and India, this 'shadow class' is that huge population who provide the low-cost labour for their industries, but cannot afford to buy their products.

To a degree, governments have recognised the problem that these inequalities now pose to the stability of the (capitalist) system. For example, the advantages of the 'automatic stabilisers' of the welfare systems of Western Europe in staving off severe deflation are widely acknowledged. But it is notable that government efforts to remedy this situation are taking place without much organised pressure from below, and are in fact jeopardised by the feebleness of collective voice. Thus, for example, in the US health reform debate, the eloquence and rationality of President Obama are having to compensate for the absence of any sufficient social coalition to impose this and other necessary reforms. In effect a large political price is now being paid for the political disenfranchisement, during the long years of neoliberal hegemony, of what used to be called the working class. The instruments of that disenfranchisement include the dissolution of many of the democratic structures of the Labour Party in Britain, and the plutocratisation of political representation in the United States.

GEOPOLITICAL DIMENSIONS OF THE CRISIS

There are also geopolitical risks in the current crisis. These arise from the changing balance of relative power between the established economies and powers of the west, and the emerging economies of China, India, Brazil, and others. We know from the experience of the 1930s that major readjustments in the relative power and prosperity of states can lead to serious conflicts between them, and to severe turbulence in their internal politics. The outcome of the great crash and the great depression was that cooperative relationships between nations largely broke down during the 1930s, in economic protectionism, ideological polarisation and world war. While this does not seem to be the destructive direction in which international relations are currently headed, one serious danger lies in the difficulties faced by the United States in negotiating, in its internal politics, an inevitable decline in its relative power. Although the recent electoral victory of Obama and the Democrats represents a source of hope, the continuing intransigence of the Republican opposition, and the possibility that a failure of the Democrats in government might bring to office a president with a political outlook like that of Sarah Palin, is a cause for concern. A substantial block of opinion in 'Middle America', urged on by its ideologues, believes that the solution to the crisis brought about by neoliberalism and by the over-reaching of American power is even more of the same. Whether in individuals, groups, or nations, the experience of downward mobility and humiliation can give rise to very destructive states of mind.

There is a further emerging crisis, arising from the multifarious consequences of climate change, which poses deep problems for the resolution of the general economic turbulence being considered here. This interconnection arises from the fact that the 'Keynesian' remedies of an increase in demand, and of a more equal pattern of consumption, on a global as well as a national scale – remedies which would 'normally' be appropriate in economic terms, and which are to some degree being followed by governments – now run up against a contrary need drastically to change current modes of consumption and production, in order to curtail discharges of carbon and other contaminating gases into the atmosphere. Here is another 'system contradiction': the need for more material outputs for one purpose is now negated by the need for lower outputs for an even more pressing reason. Although governments rightly see opportunities for new forms of production and consumption in renewable energy and energy-saving investment, the fact is that a much greater transformation in the economic system may be needed than can be achieved through growth in these sectors alone. There needs to be a major shift, in already-rich societies, in the accepted definitions of well-being, away from the production and consumption of commodities, and towards satisfactions that are less materially greedy – on a scale which is hardly yet recognised.

Gramsci showed that 'organic crises' could sometimes take many decades to resolve themselves, in situations where neither side in an underlying conflict of social forces could obtain a decisive advantage. Such a case was the French Revolution of 1789. 'A crisis appears which sometimes lasts for decades', he wrote.

> This exceptional duration means that incurable contradictions have appeared (have come to maturity) in the structure, and that the political forces working positively for the preservation and defence of the same structure are exerting themselves nevertheless to heal them within certain limits and to overcome them.[15]

This seems exactly to describe the present situation, where although there have been exceptional interventions in the economy by governments, the restoration of 'business as usual' still seems to be the overriding goal. Social forces are so finely balanced that plans for necessary reforms (for example in the finance and tax systems, or in the use and production of energy) are immobilised.

POLITICS NOW

What are the implications for British politics of these intersecting problems? What ways forwards can be expected or hoped for?

One of the larger problems is that the mentalities and expectations induced by thirty years of neoliberal dominance are now deeply ingrained, not least in many of the attitudes of the Labour government itself. The culture of individualism and inequality, the preference wherever possible for market solutions, and the dependence of the British economy on its financial sector as the leading-edge source of growth and profits, work against the solutions that are now needed. These call for a willingness to sacrifice short-term private interests for the public good, a more equal distribution of income and wealth (essential, for example, if housing is to become affordable for those on lower incomes), and the giving of greater priority to the well-being of future generations. Although Labour has of late been making some moves in a positive direction (at last, something like a radical policy on energy; a redirection of investment towards public transport proposing the replacement of much domestic air travel by high-speed trains; some recognition of the costs of neglecting the manufacturing sector; attempts to regulate financial institutions effectively; some higher taxation on the very rich), these developments do not yet amount to a coherent strategy for the redirection of the economy.

Furthermore, at the time of writing (September 2009) it seems unlikely that Labour will survive in office after the general election which is due in less than a year's time. But whatever one may think about Gordon Brown and his government, there seems virtually no respect at all in which the policies of Cameron's Tories are likely to be an improvement on Labour's. For all Cameron's presentational liberalism, it seems (increasingly) likely that a Tory government would be even more market-oriented, more inegalitarian, and more nationalist than even New Labour has been.

There is much despair about Brown's prime ministership, although one should recognise the 'over-determination' of the orchestrated denigration of him, and the exploitation of his weaknesses by those whose primary aim is to defeat Labour. Like Wilson before him, Brown is derided and feared as much because of what are believed to be his vestigial commitments to statist and egalitarian ways of thinking as for his more everyday weaknesses and failings. It is easy to be drawn into the media fixation with personality and presentation, and to be persuaded that a leader more adept in *that* dimension of politics might be an improvement from Labour's point of view. But it should be noted that in all the interminable discussions of a possible change of Labour leadership, changes in policy and direction have had no place at all, excepting only in the advocacy by ex-Blairites of a return to the even more market- and business-oriented agenda of the Blair era. In few respects do any of the mooted leadership alternatives to Brown offer an improvement to the policy agenda of his government.

But the time-frame of the British electoral cycle, and that within which the larger economic crisis is working itself out, are significantly different from each other. The general election will be decided within a year, but who can imagine that the larger crises described above will be resolved in so short a period? In this respect the crisis of the 2000s *is* like that of the 1970s – the Thatcher governments took six or seven years (and the Falklands victory) to develop and impose their radical agenda. The 'big bang' of financial deregulation took place in 1986, only after the defeat of the miners' strike in 1985. Whatever government takes office in 2010 (and in regard to that prospect Brown's resilience and far-sightedness should not be discounted), it will face severe problems which will take several years to resolve.

What have been largely 'system contradictions' may well before long take on the form of severe 'social contradictions', as governments encounter public resistance to – for example – cuts in public spending, further rises in unemployment, and other proposals for unequal sacrifices to meet the costs of recovery. A Conservative government could meet severe difficulties, and encounter disillusionment, once the novelty of a government which at any rate will offer fresh faces has worn off. There may be three or four years in which an alternative political perspective could be built, encompassing not only Labour but also the smaller parties of the centre-left (Lib Dems, Greens, Scottish and Welsh Nationalists), which might then represent a more convincing way forward out of the crisis of neoliberalism than it seems that the Cameron Tories are likely to offer. This crisis impels us to think in a time-frame longer than that of a single election.

NOTES

1. The classic text for this of kind approach is S. Hall. C. Critcher, T. Jefferson, J. Clarke and B. Roberts, *Policing the Crisis: Mugging, the State and Law and Order,* Macmillan 1978. See also the series of articles by Hall in *Marxism Today*, which can be found at http://www.amielandmelburn.org.uk/collections/mt/index_frame.htm.
2. As he put it, 'from the first moment to the last, the lonely hour of the "last instance" never comes'.

3. Althusser, through the influence of Lacan, drew on Freud's ideas of 'condensation' and 'displacement' to understand the different forms of determination and contradiction in social formations. As Ben Brewster puts it in his useful glossary for Althusser's *For Marx*, Verso 1965: 'In periods of stability the essential contradictions of the social formation are neutralised by displacement; in a revolutionary situation, however, they may condense or fuse into a revolutionary rupture.' (No better example of such a neutralising 'displacement' can be imagined than the recent diversion of public rage about the greed and irresponsibility of the bankers into the less disruptive scandal of the MPs' expenses. Indeed the expenses controversy has had the effect of weakening the agencies of government which would be indispensable to any effective constraint being set upon the financial sector.) Althusser was at pains to say that he was not interested in analogies between the substantive objects of psychoanalysis and historical materialism, but rather 'in the possibility of revealing epistemological analogies between Marx's theoretical work and Freud's' (Althusser and Balibar, *Reading Capital*, Verso 1968, p243). Laclau and Mouffe (in *Hegemony and Socialist Strategy*, Verso 1985) took up this methodological analogy through their concept of 'suture'; and Slavoj Zizek (in *The Sublime Object of Ideology*, Verso 1989, pp 87-130) has taken this much further, for example in his discussion of the Lacanian idea of 'points de capiton' (or quilting points) to understand the fixing of nodes of meaning and contradiction in the social order.

4. Ernesto Laclau and Chantel Mouffe, in *Hegemony and Socialist Strategy* and their subsequent writings, pushed this argument for the relative autonomy of the ideological and the political spheres much further, rejecting the presupposition of any ultimate determination of political outcomes by reference to economic or class structures. However, while one should not assume such determination *a priori*, this is not to say that as a matter of fact it never happens.

5. See, for example, I. Prigogine, *The End of Certainty: Time, Chaos and the New Laws of Nature*, Free Press 1996.

6. K. Dennis and J. Urry, *After the Car*, Polity 2009.

8. D. Lockwood, 'Social Integration and System Integration', in G.K. Zollschan and W. Hirsch (eds), *Explorations in Social Change*, Routledge and Kegan Paul 1964.

9. 'Ungovernability' became the theme of a large academic and political debate at that time. Two influential views of the situation were, from the left, Jurgen Habermas's *Legitimation Crisis* (1976), and Claus Offe's *Contradictions of the Welfare State* (1984); and from a different perspective, Daniel Bell's *The Cultural Contradictions of Capitalism* (1976).

10. On the falling rate of profit see P. Armstrong, A. Glyn and J. Harrison, *Capitalism since 1945*, Fontana 1984.

11. J.B. Foster and F. Magdoff (2009), *The Great Financial Crisis: Causes and Consequences*, Monthly Review Press 2009.

12. In Britain, Ann Pettifor has also argued that a deficiency of purchasing power among those on lower incomes lies at the root of the mortgage crisis and the financial havoc this has caused (see 'Bring Back Keynes', *Guardian Comment is Free*, 30.12.08). It is interesting to note that to the ethical case against the negative consequences of inequality for health and other public goods (powerfully made by Richard Wilkinson and Kate Pickett in *The Spirit Level: Why More Equal Societies Almost Always Do Better*, Allen Lane 2009) can now be added an economic case against inequality, as giving rise to a financial crisis whose origins lie in underconsumption.

13. Robin Murray has pointed out to me that it is not only underconsumption which lies at the core of this situation, but failures in the growth of production and productivity in the United States and Britain in particular. It has seemed that more money could be made in the financial sector, by avoiding the tedious constraints of manufacture and the complex social relations that technologies usually involve.

14. J. Authers, 'Long view: China's health gives rise to fresh growth theory', *Financial Times*, 5.6.09; http://www.ft.com/cms/s/0/a324a9b0-51f2-11de-b986-00144feabdc0.html.

15. Stuart Hall has reminded me of this passage – see *The Modern Prince and other writings*, Lawrence and Wishart 1957, p166.

3. What crisis is this?

John Clarke

There is widespread agreement that we are currently experiencing a crisis of substantial proportions, provoking claims that existing ways of doing things cannot go on – whether this takes the form of President Sarkozy's demand for a 'capitalism with morals' or the perceived need to restructure the regulation of the financial sector. But pushing this apparent consensus on the present-as-crisis a little further reveals a more puzzling problem – what sort of crisis is this? While everyone seems to agree on the crisis-like character of the present, hardly anyone agrees on what sort of crisis it is.

Looking across the different conceptions of crisis, it is possible to see claims that this is a crisis confined to the financial services sector, or even just to rogue elements within it. In such a view, restoring the proper balance, getting back to business as usual and ensuring the fundamental freedoms of the market from government interference are the priorities. This minimalist definition of the crisis can be juxtaposed with more epochal views, that this is a crisis of capitalism, or at least a particular phase or form of capitalism – neoliberalism, perhaps? But even those who see the crisis as one of capitalism understand this in very different ways. For some, it is the predictably disorderly conclusion of a period of dominance by (deregulated) finance capital, which has operated without any regard for the conditions of capital accumulation in the long term. For others, it is the sound of a debt and consumption driven phase of capitalism hitting the end stops of global environmental disaster. Alternatively it is seen as the crisis of neoliberalism – the radical experiment in liberating markets and capital from social and political constraints to discover – and exploit – new possibilities for capital accumulation.

I don't for a moment suppose that this brief list exhausts the different understandings of crisis that are currently in circulation. That is not my intention here. My aim is to use these different understandings to start a conversation about what sort of crisis this is – and how to think about its strange multiplicity. There is something about the present that suggests that these multiple and competing definitions of the crisis are indicative of more than a matter of different points of view: rather, they suggest that the present forms a conjuncture in which different forces, different tendencies and even different crises come together.

THE HERE AND NOW?

It seems clear that the financialisation of debt – especially 'bad' debt – was the central mechanism of the current crisis, tripping a deregulated financial sector into a series of problems that evaded both market mechanisms and the devices of self-regulation, to proliferate and extend well beyond the financial institutions. But this immediate cause has made other tendencies more visible, and more problematic. In particular the financialisation of debt is itself only one aspect of the critical relation between debt and expanded consumption in what is variously known as the neoliberal, Anglo-American or Anglo-Saxon model of capitalism. The US and the UK have been world leaders in the extension of credit as the basis for expanding domestic consumption during the boom years, and this greater indebtedness subsidised consumption even while average wages stagnated. This was the hidden core of perpetual expansion – the promise that the Anglo-American model could generate permanent growth, deliver consumer satisfaction and even overcome global poverty.

Here we can begin to see the difficulty, in thinking about the present as a conjuncture, in trying to locate it within any limited conception of the dimensions of time and space. Put simply, the present is neither just here or now. The crisis has a history (to which I will return), and it is not just a British or Anglo-American crisis – even though it has had interesting consequences for the reinvigoration of national framings of crisis. On the contrary, the development of a global economy (and a globalised financial system, in particular) means that nowhere has been immune to the dynamics and effects of the financial crisis. But nor does that make it plain and simply a 'global crisis', as if everywhere was experiencing the same dynamics and effects. Instead, both the causes and – perhaps more importantly – the consequences have been unevenly distributed, even within particular regions or political regimes (for example, the different experiences of Iceland and Norway as parts of the Nordic grouping). In the past, conjunctures have tended to be discussed in national terms – dealing with the coming together in a given space of different tendencies and sets of political forces and possibilities. For example, *Policing the Crisis* (often the reference point for conjunctural analysis) had a very specific national framing, even if it was associated with a post-colonial view of the nation.[1] This is not to argue that the nation as a focus of political analysis or political action has gone away – just that it needs to be understood as one focal point (and framing), produced out of spatial relationships that both connect and disconnect places, processes and politics.

Some of the relationships that help to constitute the (dis) United Kingdom are obvious: the 'special relationship' (and its variations) with the USA, the tangled tribulations of 'Europe' and the bitter residues of Empire. But the revelations of the financial crisis and the attempts to resolve it serve both to reinforce the importance of these relationships and to indicate other, less obvious ones – for example, the uncomfortable intersection of pension and public institutional funds with the Icelandic financial services industry; the outsourcing of both work and money to other places, notably India; and the finance driven rise of London as a world city.[2] This interwovenness of place makes the conjuncture more difficult to analyse, not least because it makes the dynamics of causes and consequences spatial, as well as economic or political. A distinctively British (English? Scottish?) form of the crisis is not simply produced by 'domestic' conditions; it is profoundly shaped by how the UK is inserted into a globalising world, not least as the adjunct to a United States whose geopolitical hegemony has proved difficult to sustain (despite a lot of time, effort and resources).

If the place of the conjuncture is difficult to analyse, then its time is equally so. These crises and contradictions have been accumulating over a much longer period than the relatively short time-scale of deregulated financialisation, or even the debt/consumption nexus central to the Anglo-American model of neoliberal growth. As a result, one issue for the analysis of the conjuncture is how different time-scales, different temporalities, or even different rhythms, happen to coincide in the 'here and now'. Certainly there are immediate causes and (relatively) short-term tendencies around the financial regime, but there are more medium-term dynamics too. The combination of deregulatory and voraciously globalising orientations that is associated with neoliberalism is part of the conditions for this crisis – both in terms of enabling the institutional dynamics of the financialisation and debt/consumption nexus and, equally importantly, in diminishing the institutional capacity of states and other public agencies to constrain or control the 'anti-social' tendencies of liberated markets.

Neoliberal political economy has contributed a series of antagonisms, contradictions and failures to the present moment of crisis (even if this may still not be a crisis of neoliberalism, see below). But neoliberalism was itself only one of the strategies associated with the crisis of Atlantic Fordism as the dominant mode of capital accumulation in the second half of the twentieth century. The crisis tendencies of the present might also be read as the failure, or the exhaustion, of many of the 'posts-' associated with the attempt to revive and renew capital accumulation during that period. For me, the most notable problems are associated with the 'post-national' strategies (responses to the current crisis have been mainly organised through nation states); 'post-statist' orientations, or at least anti-statist (states have now become favoured actors, or at least sources of funds); and 'post-welfarist' commitments (the spending of public funds on welfare has become possible and imaginable, even if much of it has been on corporate welfare). These aspects of post-Fordism have shaped the political and institutional environment for both global capital and national populations over the last four decades – creating en route some of the intellectual and political space for neoliberal political projects.

It is in this sense that the time of the present is complicated – several different time frames overlap, coalesce and produce a moment when many things appear to be broken, exhausted or deeply contradictory. Trying to work out what sort of crisis this is means trying to see how these different tendencies come together – but there are other dynamics at stake here, too.

A CRISIS OF WHAT?

So far I have followed most other commentators in identifying the elements of crisis as economic or political-economic. I am not sure that this is either entirely correct or entirely helpful. There are certainly the crisis tendencies that I have just described, but it is important to think the conjuncture rather more widely, to see just how much may be condensed into the sense of the present as a crisis. Although some political dynamics are closely related to the reconfiguration of capitalism, others appear to have a more autonomous life. Absent or anorexic public institutions have been shaped by a variety of anti-statist political projects (not just neoliberalism), while the decline of popular engagement in official politics is marked (in many countries) by a longer secular trend towards scepticism and distrust. More particularly, one might point to the conjunction of this longer political disengagement with the immediate political crisis of MPs' expenses during 2009 in the UK.

Whether this is viewed as a distraction from the 'real crisis' or as a further stage in mediated public scepticism and cynicism, it is not reducible to the economic dynamics of crisis. It has its own long- and short-term temporal specificity, and points to a problem about the place and significance of politics in the present crisis and its resolution. The popular relationship to politics also points to the return of the national as a political-cultural focus. Here, too, there are political-economic connections – most obviously, the new vulnerabilities and insecurities generated by the projects of globalisation and Europeanisation. Nevertheless, the revitalisation of nationalism – at least across most of Europe – is a distinctive political-cultural phenomenon in which postcolonial legacies meet a variety of other elements – anti-Muslim orientalism, anti-migrant localism, and the reinvention of nationality as a claims-making identity.

Finally, there are other social dynamics in which a variety of economic, political and cultural tendencies (and antagonisms) are compressed and condensed. For instance, a cosmopolitan conception of consumption encounters 'moral' objections, ranging from the defence of 'traditional' roles and identities to the elaboration of models of ethical consumption or a global anti-globalisation. In the UK particularly, the liberalisation of trade, commerce and consumption (e.g. in changes to licensing laws around alcohol, sex clubs and gambling) encountered – but overrode – multiple sources of opposition, while being accompanied by a massive legislative programme of criminalisation that sought to control disorderly and anti-social behaviour and people. Such persistent and paradoxical crises of morality (and authority, perhaps) seem an integral part of the present – not least because of New Labour's combination of economic liberalisation and social authoritarianism.

Perhaps nowhere is this moral instability more visible than in the question of reward. Since the mid-1970s, the possibility of public intervention into the distribution of income and wealth has seemed impossible, as successive governments have insisted on reward being determined by market forces – a recurrent theme in relation to executive salaries and bonuses (not only in the financial sector). Elsewhere, however, New Labour have continuously stressed the virtues of hard work (the central discursive figure of New Labour is the 'hard-working family'); summoning 'responsible citizens' to take on more and more responsibilities (particularly those that government has no interest in performing) has been unequally targeted – persistently addressed to the vulnerable rather than the powerful. And here there has been no political engagement with the older moral (and Old Labour) questions of desert and reward, except of course in relation to those despised sections of the non-working population. Consequently, the symbolism of the financial sector's 'bonus culture' (and subsequent 'rewards for failure') could have been significant popular issues, but ruling governments (and oppositions) have had little political purchase on them. Indeed, such potential sites of popular political realignment have been largely ignored (and subsequently fed back into the anger about MPs' expenses).

In such ways, the conjuncture needs to be seen as more than the maturing of economic or political-economic contradictions. The social remains a field of unresolved antagonisms, in which governmental efforts to 'modernise the people' alongside the globalisation of the economy have been halting, contradictory and (above all) authoritarian in tone and substance.

CRISIS TALK AND CRISIS MANAGEMENT

The other important dynamic in the present is that, as I noted at the beginning, almost everyone sees this as a crisis – not just critical or progressive commentators. Indeed the competition to name the crisis, to identify its distinctive characteristics and treat it as the ground on which to demand new ways of doing things is intense. Crisis talk has been dominated by what might best be described as restorationist governmental approaches, however, whose primary commitments have been to re-establish the conditions for 'business as usual'. Despite the rhetorical flourishes (promises of a global new deal, or a new capitalism with morals), the main result has been the massive public subsidy paid to failing financial institutions to ensure that the 'system' is saved. Three features of this restorationist dynamic stand out for me: the nationalisation of crisis, the revival of the state, and the significance of crisis time.

Although the crisis is widely constructed as a 'global' one, the dominant definitions have inscribed it in national terms (referencing 'our' banks, industries, people). Similarly, the main policy responses – financial subsidies, government intervention, the remaking of regulation – have also tended to be framed in terms of national political decision-making (albeit with some regional and international collaborations and tensions). This national construction easily slides into a variety of anti-global and anti-European nationalisms (most obviously around that troublesome and mobile conception of 'British jobs for British workers'). But the effect of internationalising capital accumulation means that it is ever more difficult to identify the nationality of capital, corporations – or banks.

The nationalisation of the crisis is intimately bound up with the revived role for the state as the guarantor of last resort. The sudden enthusiasm for public intervention, public spending, and a willingness to be dependent on public funds, is perverse and paradoxical. But it should not be surprising: the rhetorical anti-statism of neoliberal and neoconservative politics was rarely reflected in governmental practice. On the contrary, states were 're-tooled' and made more effective contributors to corporate welfare in various ways. The crisis has seen this corporate welfare role expand on a dramatic scale, it is true, but the binary opposition of state versus market was rarely an adequate guide for political analysis. Nevertheless, this dramatic expansion has put into play new problems and contradictions about the relationship between public and private interests, which will continue to reverberate as the 'bill' for the rescue package takes its toll on the possibilities for public or collective well-being over the next decade or more.

But crisis talk was also significant in another way – it enabled the restorationist and interventionist programmes of different governments to be pressed through under the sign of 'crisis'. Other perspectives and other time frames (the ecological time frame, questions of adequate housing, the control of international capital) were overshadowed by the announced immediacy and urgency of the crisis itself – and the imperative demand that it be resolved. The crisis was presented as a state of emergency, and such emergencies demand 'fast policy'. For example, the prospect of 'melt-down' in the global web of finance capital (and its 'established' names and institutions) prompted demands for immediate action on the part of governments. The urgency was established in part in the name of restoring the future: the crisis threatened the possibility of an orderly transition to an imagined future – a future centrally imagined as 'more of the same'. Discontinuity, rupture, and the threatened prospect of system failure represented the loss of a future in which we were all presumed to be invested (materially or emotionally).

Crises always emerge as constructed, narrated and temporalised events and times. It is impossible to arrive at an 'innocent' view of crisis, since crises are always already defined and constructed as (potentially) governable objects. The recent crisis emerged as the focus of governmental and political narratives that included the projected state-of-emergency timeframe and the demand that 'something must be done'. No longer, as Foucault might have said, is this a claim that 'society must be defended': it is the financial system – or the economy – that must be saved (if necessary from itself). This crisis time also summons and empowers would-be managers or governors of the crisis – those who can intervene to protect, defend or restore.

All of this reminded me that Gramsci once argued that: 'it may be ruled out that immediate economic crises of themselves produce fundamental historical events; they can simply create a terrain more favourable to the dissemination of certain modes of thought, and certain ways of posing and resolving questions'.[3] The crisis has certainly made it possible to pose alternative questions – about the failures of finance-led capitalism, deregulation and the globalisation of capital accumulation. It has made it more possible to disseminate other modes of thought – about the value of states, about questions of social security, about the significance of interdependence, and about the ecological implications of continually expanding consumption.

Nevertheless, these remain alternative modes of thought and questions, rather than the dominant ones. While the crisis has enabled their circulation, the present – at least in Europe – feels dominated by restorationist, if not regressive, modes of thought in economic, political and social domains.

THE CRISIS OF POLITICS AND THE POLITICS OF CRISIS

In a recent book about publicness, Janet Newman and I have explored questions of de-politicisation in relation to public policy.[4] Two issues stand out in this context. The first concerns the problem of politics itself. Although the crisis may have made it more possible to pose alternative questions and solutions – and to demand a progressive politics to move beyond this crisis (and its potential recurrence), such demands encounter the paradox of popular views of politics. Popular scepticism and cynicism about 'actually existing politics' is a difficult challenge for those of us who want to argue for a progressive politics. Persuading people to suspend their scepticism, to suggest that our politics is different, or that all politics (and politicians) are not necessarily corrupt, collusive, power-obsessed and fundamentally unpleasant, is a major challenge. Where we might wish to restore politics, many people wish to avoid it. Ordinary people, in this sense, are understood as being both above and below politics – above because they transcend the narrow, self-interested or dogmatically ideological character of politics; below because they are grounded in more practical or everyday concerns. I do not mean that this view of ordinary people is true – it is a characteristically populist juxtaposition of the people against the political class/the elite. But survey after survey (and evidence of declining political participation rates in many places) suggests that it is at least partly – and contingently – true.

However, this anti-politics view of politics co-exists in paradoxical ways with other desires and anxieties that demand public and political solutions, and this is the second issue: public doubt about the efficacy of politics co-exists with a desire for it to address our anxieties and insecurities in an uncertain world. Unfortunately, current solutions to the crisis are likely to make things worse on these issues rather than better. The material and emotional dynamics of security and uncertainty have been grasped by UK governments mainly in terms of policies against terrorism and anti-social behaviour. And this narrow view of security has meant that matters of economic, environmental and social security have been 'devolved' to become the responsibilities of would-be entrepreneurial citizens and their 'hard working families'.

This mixture of popular desires and doubts is a profoundly unstable one, and at present appears vulnerable to being captured by varieties of nationalist and racialised imaginaries of exclusion – excluding others or excluding ourselves from the larger world. The challenge for a progressive politics is to be able to address such desires and doubts in ways that build interdependencies and solidarities rather than exclusions. But the solutions to the crisis that have been put forward by government – and their economic, social and political costs – have if anything intensified the doubts, while frustrating the desires. In particular, the public has been summoned to play its part in these solutions in the most de-politicising and de-mobilising ways.

Different publics have had to be negotiated and addressed – spoken of, and spoken to – in the various circulating narratives of crisis.[5] As I indicated earlier, these publics appear to be profoundly sceptical or cynical. (I suspect they always were in some measure – existing in conditions of what I have called passive dissent, or what Jeremy Gilbert has strikingly referred to as 'disaffected consent'.) Dominant political strategies for addressing these public paradoxes have oscillated between the technical and the emotional. On the one hand, we have seen heavy emphasis on the fiscal and regulatory techniques and technologies necessary to restore business as usual. On the other, government has addressed the public as emotional or affective entities: states of anxiety, insecurity, outrage, scepticism and more have been addressed, attributed and folded into governmental stories. Perhaps the most striking feature of the discourses about publicness in the crisis is that publics have been summoned to perform the most abject role: their identity is almost entirely enfolded into the problem of public debt. These publics – and future publics – are being summoned to pay the costs of corporate welfare (saving the system) while being told that the public services on which their own welfare might depend will be retrenched again to balance the public books.

It is important to recognise the ways in which these 'emotional' publics might outrun governmental attempts to contain or appropriate them. The collective combination of desires and doubts have produced frustrations, anxieties and anger that have been focused on very diverse and heterogeneous targets: bankers, governments, migrant workers, and 'the system' itself. How might this turbulent mixture be articulated with a more progressive way of 'posing and answering questions'?

NOTES

1. S. Hall, C. Critcher, J. Jefferson, J. Clarke, and B. Roberts, *Policing the Crisis: Mugging, the State and Law and Order*, Macmillan 1978.
2. D. Massey, *World City*, Polity Press 2007.
3. A. Gramsci, *Selections from the Prison Notebooks* (edited by G. Nowell-Smith), Lawrence and Wishart 1971, p184.
4. J. Newman and J. Clarke, *Publics, Politics and Power: remaking the public in public services*, Sage 2009.
5. See the suggestive comments by Grahame Thompson, 'How the financial crisis is being packaged for public consumption' (2009); http://www.open.ac.uk/ccig/dialogues/blogs/how-the-financial-crisis-is-being-packaged-for-public-consumption.

4. INTERPRETING THE CRISIS

Stuart Hall & Doreen Massey

Doreen There are many different ways of thinking about the current crisis, but certainly one useful way is to think about the present as a conjuncture – this way of analysing was very productive in the discussions about Thatcherism in the late 1970s and 1980s in *Marxism Today* and elsewhere, in which you played a leading role.[1] Perhaps we should start by thinking about what conjunctural analysis is, and how it differs from other kinds of analysis.

Stuart It's partly about periodisation. A conjuncture is a period when different social, political, economic and ideological contradictions that are at work in society and have given it a specific and distinctive shape come together, producing a crisis of some kind. The post-war period, dominated by the welfare state, public ownership and wealth redistribution through taxation was one conjuncture; the neoliberal, market-forces era unleashed by Thatcher and Reagan was another. These are two distinct conjunctures, separated by the crisis of the 1970s. A conjuncture can be long or short: it's not defined by time or by simple things like a change of regime – though these have their own effects. As I see it, history moves from one conjuncture to another rather than being an evolutionary flow. And what drives it forward is usually a crisis, when the contradictions that are always at play in any historical moment are condensed, or, as Althusser said, 'fuse in a ruptural unity'. Crises are moments of potential change, but the nature of their resolution is not given. It may be that society moves on to another version of the same thing (Thatcher to Major?), or to a somewhat transformed version (Thatcher to Blair); or relations can be radically transformed.

Gramsci and Althusser, who helped us to think in this way, were primarily interested in such moments of major ruptural crisis (like 1917), when the 'organic' relations of society – especially the economic structure – were deeply reshaped. Gramsci thought the conjunctural level less significant than the organic. But he does also talk about using the notion of conjuncture in a broader, more methodological way: as a way of marking significant transitions between different political moments; that is to say, to apply it as a general system of analysis to any historical situation. And that is how I use it now. In *Policing the Crisis* we tried to look at the postwar period, which – despite its many contradictory aspects – was a conjuncture dominated by what has been called the post-war, social-democratic consensus. This political 'settlement' came apart in the crisis upheavals of the 1970s. Thatcherism, neoliberalism, globalisation, the era dominated by market forces, brutally 'resolved' the contradictions and opened a new conjuncture.

The question is, can we look at the present situation in that way? When does it begin? Has it been through a crisis before? What sort of crisis is this? Is it temporary? Is it going to transform things but not very deeply, followed by a return to 'business as usual'? Is it what is called a passive revolution, when none of the social forces are able to enforce their political will and things go stumbling along in an unresolved way? John Major's government was such a moment, when things that had been inaugurated by Thatcherism were in serious difficulties, but were patched together by the dominant classes, to hold the Tories in power for a few more years, without any serious challenge from below

Doreen One of the reasons for needing to understand the structural character of the current conjuncture is that, as you say, it's not predetermined what the outcome will be, or what will happen. And this kind of analysis gives us some purchase on understanding the range of potential outcomes.

Stuart I agree. It forces you to look at many different aspects, in order to see what the balance of social forces is and how you might intervene, or have a better idea of how to intervene effectively. So is this crisis about a real shift in the balance of social forces? Or, if not, how can we push the crisis from a compromise ending to a more radical rupture, or even a revolutionary resolution? But first you have to analyse ruthlessly what sort of crisis it is.

Doreen The other thing that's really striking – and I went back as you have been doing and looked at the *Prison Notebooks*, and Althusser – is the importance of thinking of things as complex moments, where different parts of the overall social formation may themselves, independently, be in crisis in various ways, but at a certain point they are condensed. Although we see this moment as a big economic crisis, it is also a philosophical and political crisis in some ways – or it could be, if we got hold of the narrative. So it's really important that we don't only 'do the economy', as it were.

Stuart Absolutely not. It is not a moment to fall back on economic determinism, though it may be tempting to do so, since the current crisis seems to start in the economy, with the collapse of the global financial system and the banks. But any serious analysis of the crisis must take into account its other 'conditions of existence'. For example, the ideological – the way market fundamentalism has become the economic common sense, not only of the west but globally; politically – the way New Labour has been disconnected from its political roots and evolved as the second party of capital, transforming the political terrain; socially – the way class and other social relations have been so reconfigured under consumer capitalism that they fragment, undermining the potential social constituencies or agencies for change.

Gramsci, who struggled all life against 'economism', was very clear about this. What he says is that no crisis is only economic. It is always 'over-determined' from different directions. On the other hand, you can't think about a crisis and its resolution until you deal with what he calls the economic nucleus. We can't ignore the way the financial sector has asserted its dominance over the economy as a whole, or indeed its centrality to the new forms of global capitalism. But we must address the complexity of the crisis as a whole. This is a difficult balance, but, as you say, crises are always 'over-determined'. Different levels of society, the economy, politics, ideology, common sense, etc, come together or 'fuse'. Otherwise, you could get an unresolved ideological crisis which doesn't have immediate political connotations, or which you can't see as being directly related to a change in the economy. The definition of a conjunctural crisis is when these 'relatively autonomous' sites – which have different origins, are driven by different contradictions, and develop according to their own temporalities – are nevertheless 'convened' or condensed in the same moment. Then there is crisis, a break, a 'ruptural fusion'.

Doreen As you were speaking, I was thinking that maybe one of the things that they – the Tories, the neoliberals, including New Labour – have managed to do is almost to separate the economic crisis from the philosophical one. There was a period, when the financial crisis was first in the news, when people were beginning to question the way they were thinking about the economy and consider alternative ways of doing things – for example there was a discernible shift to investing more in the co-op, talking about mutualisation, arguing that we need to get rid of all this individualism and greed. And yet today here we are sitting here with Cameron saying that the big problem is the public deficit, and the big state. The economic crisis is partly being solved, at least for the time being, and that is seen as the only problem. The implosion of neoliberal ideology is no longer on the agenda. It's as though they've separated those two instances again.

Stuart For a brief moment some people did indeed say 'this economic model isn't working any more'. But the separation between the economic and the ideological seems to have reasserted itself. This has been characteristic of our whole period. From very early on, New Labour said, really, there are no major ideological or economic questions left; there is only 'managing society'. In this latter respect, New Labour's neoliberalism differed from Thatcher's – though they remained variants of the same thing. Thatcherism was anti-state, whereas New Labour made a 'rediscovery' of 'active government'. New Labour said that they could do marketisation better than the Tories, who were running into trouble, and could avoid a huge political backlash by blurring the private/public divide, and letting the market buy out most of the public activities that were profitable, while the state concentrated on the technical management of the consequences. New Labour was very successful in boxing up that whole question in this way – one which didn't seem to offer an ideological or political choice. What began to happen – certainly in the moment of the downturn and perhaps a bit before that – is that some of these connections began to come to the surface. But there has been a failure by Labour to address them or to find a way of narrativising them into a crisis of the whole system. Since New Labour shares with the financial sector a view about how critical it is for the global capitalist system to continue to work, they are satisfied to say, 'In the long run, everything depends on getting back to business as usual'.

Doreen And we can distract attention by having the ministers and the parliamentarians taken to task over expenses and suchlike. *They* become the bogeys, not the bankers.

Stuart Politics is often the source of a spectacle designed to divert you from what is really important. The furore over MPs' expenses was really an instance of that. Of course, in an era when New Labour 'is extremely relaxed about people becoming filthy rich', MPs will put their snouts in the trough too. But I'm sure most of the deep public feeling, the slightly irrational anger, about MPs' expenses is because people can't get at the culprits. Indeed, many people have no real idea what it is like to be really filthy rich in our society. The people who know are the bankers, the top CEOs, the hedge-fund managers who operate globally, bank off-shore, live an extravagant lifestyle without limits and pay themselves exorbitant salaries and bonuses for getting things disastrously wrong. But the anger becomes displaced onto MPs – which is not to deny that some of them behaved in a shamefully greedy way.

Doreen I agree with that, and I think there's another reason, which is that we pay the MPs and are therefore entitled to criticise them – they are in some sense accountable to us. Whereas the bankers are part of this thing called market forces, and it is now embedded deeply within us, precisely as a result of the past thirty years, to think of market forces as somehow natural, and not criticisable in a simple way – morally, ethically, politically. We experience the financial system as being beyond any possibility of intervention. That's part of what is so disabling, precisely the ideological moment in the politics that we've inherited.

Stuart I think the ideological dimension is very critical – the way in which the whole political discourse has been 'cleansed', so that the public interest, public ownership, common goods, equality, the redistribution of wealth, the stubborn facts about poverty and inequality, etc, all became 'unspeakable'. That's an instance of the way ideology, through erasure, provides one of the conditions of existence of politics and the economy, and thus of the crisis. Thatcherism made it part of common sense that you can't calculate the common interest. 'There is no such thing as society'. All you can calculate is individual self-interest, and then the hidden hand of the market will make that work for, or trickle down to, society as a whole. The big shift here, of course, is that this has become New Labour's philosophy too.

Doreen It's become deep within individual people's philosophy – 'you can't do anything about it, it's the market, isn't it?'. It's right at the heart of the way in which we look at the world.

Stuart It operates both at the level of common sense and at what Gramsci called the level of philosophy, i.e. the new win-win economics, the mathematical formulae which tell investors how to make money out of making money, the illusion that it's an economy in which everyone profits. Gramsci would say that a hegemonic settlement only works when ideology captures or 'hegemonises' common sense; when it becomes so taken-for-granted that its ways of looking at the world seem to be the only ways in which ordinary people can calculate what's good and what's not, what they should support and what they shouldn't, what's good for them and what's good for society.

Doreen Before we speak, before we think, it's the framework within which we think.

Stuart Exactly. But I don't think the governing philosophy always become common sense. It takes a while, and a mastery of the political field. Hegemony is something which has to be struggled for, which is always in process.

Doreen It takes a huge amount of work. And quite explicit work. And they know they need to do it. When I was researching the City of London, the finance centre, I was amazed by the amount of stuff they produced.[2] Reports, pieces of research, interviews on the radio, the television, everywhere, to convince us that without them we are all dead. That they are the golden goose of the economy. They're doing the same now, with seeking to divide private sector workers from public sector workers. Labour does not put in that effort to create shifts in people's hearts and minds. It just listens to focus groups. It doesn't itself go out and try and create a new common sense, a new narrative – partly because it doesn't want to, but also …

Stuart … I don't think it knows what it would be possible to create a new common sense around.

Doreen It's got so used to having a so-called 'natural base', that it doesn't know how to create one through its own efforts. Perhaps this is the point at which to say more about hegemony, a concept that is associated with thinking about conjunctures, and those periods where there's a particular political settlement.

Stuart Not every political force or philosophy which is dominant at a particular period achieves widespread consent. It is not always the case that the governing political philosophy is spoken by everybody as if they're already inside it. It is when it becomes 'just how things are' that it wins consent and enters common sense. And at that point the political regime or philosophy has achieved a more settled, long-term, deeper form of control. It is possible to rule if you operate in a dominative way, if you tell people what to do, if you do the propaganda, if you send into labour camps people who don't agree with you, if you police the boundaries. But hegemony is much deeper than that. And I think what is so critical in understanding how hegemony is secured is to see how it makes, for example, the language of class, which we were accustomed to use, seem no longer applicable. That's not because class is unimportant or has disappeared, or because the class structure hasn't changed, or anything like that. But when you look at the theatre of politics, classes don't appear in their already-united form. Unifying them with other social forces into a 'historical bloc' is part of what politics does. The ways in which people and groups are articulated into a hegemonic project are immensely complex. If finance capital drives industrial capital to the wall, well, can we still speak of Capital as a unified entity? Some working-class people resisted Thatcherism, but some jumped on their bikes and became self-employed. Where is 'class consciousness' then? Hegemony is about winning consent through the complex articulations of different social forces that do not necessarily correspond to simple class terms.

Doreen And it's about that kind of interpellation of people's interests into your story. And Cameron can be seen to be making efforts to do that, you can see it in a lot of his language. And something like Thatcher's allowing people to buy their council houses was a perfect mode of drawing people in.

Stuart And on and on and on. That work has to be done so it can reach a level of unconsciousness where people aren't aware that they're speaking ideology at all. The ideology has become 'naturalised', simply part of nature. 'Market forces' was a brilliant linguistic substitute for 'the capitalist system', because it erased so much, and, since we all use the market every day, it suggests that we all somehow already have a vested interest in conceding everything to it. It conscripted us. Now, when you get to that point, the political forces associated with that project, and the philosophical propositions that have won their way into common sense, are very tough to dislodge – you can't just vote them out, or kick them out of power.

Doreen And it's not simply a matter of logic either. You have to have an alternative appeal.

Stuart You have to have an alternative popular appeal – partly because ideology is never just rubbish, it always has a basis in real things. People know that a lot of the nationalised industries were extremely inefficient and, in their own way, some of the privatised industries were more efficient. Of course, there are social costs to that. But nobody talks about the costs. They just talk about 'efficiency'. What drove that shift? Constantly associating 'the market' with positive things like freedom, choice – and thus the necessity of a privatised economy; that's the logic. You can see these chains of connection being forged in people's everyday thought and language, as well as in political debate and argument, in media discussion and in theory. People have lost a sense of where the discourse came from and what it leaves out. And when that happens, they can be seen as being subjected to the discourse. New Labour knew all about that. The logic of 'spin' was to detach concepts from their previous associations and shift them to new meanings. You can also see this process when they banished 'equality' from the vocabulary and started to talk about fairness; when they banished 'capital' and started to talk about free markets; when they gave up on 'society' and started to use that weasel word 'community' instead. All these shifts of language were ways of deconstructing a form of consciousness which had governed political thinking on the left for a long time.

Doreen Insidious little shifts from all kinds of points.

Stuart So conjunctural analysis also means describing this kind of complex field of power and consent, and looking at its different levels of expression – political, ideological, cultural and economic. It's about trying to see how all of that is deployed in the form of power which 'hegemony' describes.

Doreen So when we're thinking for instance about culture in the UK today, we should be analysing it in that way, trying to think through the ways in which it's been enrolled into the establishment of a particular kind of common sense.

Stuart Think of how the celebrity culture has co-opted ordinary people into the belief that they too can be wealthy and famous. This has very real consequences for how you make a conjunctural analysis of the present. There is a temptation – because it's the finance sector that has collapsed, thrown us into the crisis – to say, oh well, in the end 'it's the economy stupid': as if the economy determines in a simple way. But if you just look at that, and left out these other conditions which make it possible, you wouldn't really understand how power is working in this situation, and what is coming into crisis.

Doreen Nor would you give yourself all the possible fronts to work on.

Stuart Yes, of course. Because as soon as you understand why they're 'leading' in this way, you can see not only where but how a counter-intervention should be made. For instance, unless you are really prepared to deconstruct the notion that market forces defend individual freedom, and are the most efficient ways of organising economic life, unless you unpick that market thing which holds together a whole set of understandings which structure institutional life, the economy, everyday thinking, common sense, you are unlikely to be able to intervene effectively in a radical or decisive way.

Doreen Do you think, though, that finance is crucial to the conjuncture that we've just been through – if it's ended? Is the finance constellation at the nucleus of the kind of hegemony that we've seen during the last thirty years or so? I think it is, and that certain ways of thinking have come from it. In a number of ways.

Stuart I certainly think it is. My understanding of the current conjuncture is that it begins with the collapse of the welfare state and Keynesian demand-management, and all of the thinking that went with that. That phase was dominated by trying to increase the productivity of the manufacturing economy – Wilson's 'white heat of technology', 'workers by hand and brain', the capital-labour corporatist management of the state. Labour's last gasp. The 1970s is a period of upheaval, and Thatcherism resolves that crisis into a new conjuncture. The new market-forces conjuncture has two phases to it: the Thatcherite destruction of everything associated with the welfare state, letting market forces rip, privatising the state, high unemployment, and battering society as a whole into the acceptance of a new order. Then, when even the Tories think this can't work for much longer, funnily enough, a transformed and deeply co-opted New Labour provides that other, more human, face. But the two phases should be regarded as a single conjuncture which we can characterise as the triumph of neo-liberalism. I know it's an inadequate word, but it's the only one we have for characterising what defines the whole arc. Whether finance capital is so dominant in the first period, I'm not sure.

Doreen I was working in the GLC at that time. And the debates within our bit of the GLC, our arguments about what we should do, were very much concerned with the question of the future of London, and of course, one issue was London as a financial city; and what was going on during the early period of Thatcherism was the disruption of the manufacturing base, in very serious ways. That and the Big Bang. At least some of the preconditions for the shift in the economy were laid down at that time.

Stuart I think that's very important. The triumph of finance capital over industrial capital has been going since the 1970s; it also has a long history before that. Remember the dominance of finance capital and the City in the 1890s and its connection with the 'high noon' of imperialist expansion? The dominance of finance capital seems to be deeply inscribed in old and new forms of capitalist globalisation.

Doreen Yes, it's a longer history. You and I remember Harold Wilson's attempt to set up a national plan for manufacturing and labour, and when he tried to set up a Department of Economic Affairs. And what happened? It all got completely wiped out, because in the end what matters is finance. And that has been part of a two-century long history in this country, if not more. But during this last period, the thirty years, forty years, that we're talking about, the dominance, and the *nature* of the dominance, of finance – partly because of decline of manufacturing – has been sharper and different. And also, crucially, as you say, it has become more global.

Stuart So, in the story, we'd have to distinguish those two things – the central place of finance and financial investment in the City generally, and then what is distinctive about the way finance capital emerges as the centrepiece – at the expense of other elements of capital itself – in the period of globalisation since Thatcherism. Capitalism may, at the simplest level, be one thing, but it has its conjunctures too, and the analysis requires this kind of historical specificity.

Doreen Yes, and there is work going on in this area, and I think we should bring it into our political analysis. Some of this work concerns the way in which – partly because of the absence suddenly of manufacturing as a voice, and of the trade unions also – the pure matter of exchange, rather than production for the market, became the most important thing. But we should also understand that what the City – capital C – grew fat on wasn't actually globalisation, it was privatisation, and deregulation. Who benefited from the privatisation of pensions? Who benefited massively from all the contracting out, and the PPIs, PFIs and whatever they were called? And so there was an articulation in the City of a particular kind of economic thinking that – though in broad terms it is like any kind of capitalism – has a sharper focus in finance, and doesn't have to deal with nuts and bolts and widgets and textiles and mining. It's a pure form of exchange in some senses.

Stuart It's a sort of exchange out of exchange out of exchange: making money out of making money. It hardly touches ground – what people used to call 'the real economy'. Every now and again, these calculations touch reality momentarily, and then they're off again. But isn't it also important to look at the way in which finance has come to govern the whole economy, not just the City? The whole global corporate world has become much more oriented towards finance because globalisation depends so much on the transnational flow of capital, the new global division of labour and the spatial separation of investment and consumption from production.

Doreen And the manufacturing corporations themselves also operate as finance companies. Their cash-flows and their cash-holdings, and the way in which they operate, also has that mindset within it.

Stuart This dominance makes it perfectly clear why, then, if something goes wrong in that sphere, it's going to radiate out and affect all the others.

Doreen And why potentially – let's hope it does – it could blow the ideological side apart as well. But that's what's being covered up at the moment, that's where we've got to go for it.

Stuart There was a brief moment when the crisis of the neoliberal, Washington-consensus economic model was perfectly clear. Suddenly the clouds parted and people saw – not just the greed, and a new international superclass growing fat on this body of exchange – they saw something about the market: markets don't correct themselves; they don't allocate in the most efficient way; they aren't the site of equality and freedom. And ultimately the state had to come to the rescue of capital. And yet if you put those things into an alternative narrative, it doesn't seem to be going anywhere. It's all too familiar, to anybody on the left. Why then hasn't that narrative taken off?

Doreen Perhaps part of the problem *is* that the left has been saying some of these things for so long. But analysing it and knowing it ourselves is not enough. How do we get it into public debate? Where are the social forces that could take it on? The Labour Party is totally incapable of doing this. It has bought into the neoliberal narrative. So it's not prepared to do it. As we said before, it doesn't know how to do it.

narrative debate

Stuart And also, I think it sees those forces as more permanent than the crisis. For them, the crisis will pass but finance capital will live on.

Doreen And Labour has really bought into the idea that finance is our strong economic card. Rather than being – in its present form – a force for destruction, both within the country and in the world at large. It still really thinks it's the golden goose.

Stuart But what about globalisation? That is part of the picture too. Immanuel Wallerstein once argued that the inroads which the redistribution of wealth and the growing strength of labour made into the rate of profitability and capital's right to manage in the 1970s obliged capital to find alternative routes out; and its resolution, with the rise of the multinational corporation, was to 'go global'.

Doreen When we were thinking about this kind of analysis at the beginning of the Thatcher period, our analysis remained largely national – that's how we thought about hegemony, and there were real reasons for doing so. But we cannot do that now. And the change is not just one of empirical focus: globalisation means that the whole concept of hegemony no longer operates in quite the same way.

Stuart I agree with you that hegemony in the Gramscian sense has to be rethought in a situation that goes beyond the national. And I'm not sure that it's easy to talk about that, although when I think of what has established the leadership position of the United States in the new global system – ideologically, culturally, economically, militarily and in some ways politically – I think there is a way of seeing how that operates globally. But I was really thinking about whether globalisation is also a dimension of why the finance element has been so powerful.

Doreen I think it is an element, and Britain has been massively important within the construction of that, especially with the role of the City in introducing privatisation around the world – all those folk from here and the United States that went over to Moscow and told them that democracy was equivalent to marketisation.

Stuart One of the ways in which the dominance of finance is connected to globalisation is through the social division of labour, whereby the financial power remains at the centre of the 'developed' world, and continues to accumulate capital there, while much of the physical production of goods and resources takes place in the developing world. That new division of labour inevitably increases the dominance of finance capital.

Doreen What also interests me is that, even if finance capital is not going to be knocked off its perch, it is clear that the crisis in some ways has given a further impetus to what was already happening, and that is a fracturing of US hegemony and economic dominance. China and Russia are doing different things. It may still be capitalism, but it isn't simply neoliberal capitalism. There's the G20 now asserting itself, the BRIC countries asserting themselves. There isn't a single voice dominating everything. And there are the positive alternatives – with very different voices coming up in Latin America, from Lula to Morales. So things are much more uneven and differentiated. And there are lots of campaigns that are trying to address what the City does around the world, so there are things happening here too. And that takes us back to social forces – the Labour Party's not going to give us a lead on this.

Stuart I agree. Nevertheless, the Labour Party remains an important arena where these contradictory things are worked out, so we can't ignore it. It dominates the political terrain in which you have to operate; it is one critical site, because it is a kind of nodal point in the overall balance of social and political forces. For good or ill, it is still central to British politics. The argument about social forces is often read as if the Labour is so co-opted that it doesn't matter what happens to it.

Doreen We have to address it. It is there, it's the elephant in the room. But it is also important to look out beyond parliamentary and party politics to recognise the potential of social forces. An obvious case in point at the moment is the green movement.

Stuart I agree that the green/climate/environmental issue is one of the places where you're likely to find many of those non-traditional social forces. There's a big movement there and it's had an impact on common sense. It's even having an impact on political policy, and it also has an edge against market fundamentalism.

Doreen And the Green New Deal is interesting in the context of this conversation in a number of ways. Firstly, it talks about a multiplicity of crises – financial, oil and climate change crises – slightly differently from the way we are thinking about it, but nonetheless that's really quite important. Secondly, although only schematically, it tries to point to all the different social groups that are worst affected, particularly by finance, all the kind of classic potential social forces that you might think of, though articulated in different ways – social movements, and not just trade unions but also small business, and manufacturing, local-based manufacturing, stuff like that. And I just find that it's the only place I've really seen somebody even schematically trying to think through what kind of an alliance might be stitched together through common interests against the kind of nexus of politics, philosophy and economics that we've had for the last thirty to forty years.

NOTES

1. This discussion is part of an ongoing *Soundings* project to understand the current situation from the point of view of conjunctural analysis. See John Clarke, 'What crisis is this?' Chapter 3, and Mike Rustin, 'Reflections on the present', Chapter 2; and discussions from the *Soundings* 'credit crunch' seminar. For Stuart Hall's essays from *Marxism Today* see www. amielandmelburn.org.uk/collections/mt/index_frame.htm. A key text in the development of this kind of analysis was *Policing the Crisis: Mugging, the State and Law and Order*, by S. Hall, C. Critcher, J. Jefferson, J. Clarke and B. Roberts, Macmillan 1978. For further useful background reading see Gramsci, *Selections from the Prison Notebooks*, Lawrence and Wishart 1971; and Althusser, *For Marx*, Verso 1965.
2. D. Massey, *World City*, Polity Press 2007.

5. THE POLITICAL STRUGGLE AHEAD

Doreen Massey

BEYOND ECONOMICS

It is not so very long ago that the implosion that began in August 2007 looked to be bringing into question far more than the iniquities, and the dominance, of the financial sector. It seemed that there might just be the beginnings of a fracturing of elements of the hegemonic common sense. The basic tenets of market fundamentalism were found to be wanting. Even in the most 'popular' of discussion fora there was outright hostility, not just to individual bankers, but to greed and self-interest as the means by which they were seen to have risen, and now to have fallen. There were not a few who proclaimed that this looked set to be 'the end of neoliberalism'.

This was not, then, a moment of potential crisis just about finance, or even about economic theory. It ran more deeply than that. It was about a way of being human. It came near to questioning the wider hegemonic ideological framing of life. It touched upon the ethical.

That moment of potentially wider rupture has, for the moment, passed. And one of the ways in which this cover-up has been achieved is through a re-separation of the sphere of 'the economic' from the sphere of ideology (and thus, in a wider sense, of politics). This is in fact a *re*-separation. It is in itself a crucial part of a return to business as usual. For that separation has been one of the fundamental achievements of the last thirty years – the period we have come to call neoliberal. The economic has come to be viewed as a set of forces equivalent to a machine, or to the laws of nature. Its construction through social relations, and thus through potentially *different* social relations, has been hidden from view. That moment of clarity, when the economic and the ideological were fleetingly seen to be interwoven (not the same, but connected) was thus a real (potential) dislocation. For now, normality (the normality of the last thirty years) has been restored. The crisis is once again interpreted as purely financial and, crucially, as a technical question. But only for now; it is not over yet.

The June 2010 emergency budget made this plain. It was moulded by politics and ideology. It was in no sense technically 'unavoidable'. Any serious response from the left must address it at this level. Argue the case in terms of economic logic (the danger of double-dip recession, etc), yes; but also insist on the bigger picture – the ideological dimensions of this moment. If a wider break with the past is to be won, then the question of the economy has to be set within its wider conjunctural context.[1] It must address directly the ideological under-pinnings that have, until recently, been so successful and so self-assured.

It is not so long ago that this self assurance – this class victory – seemed to be a simple fact of life. Andrew Adonis and Stephen Pollard, for example, argued that:

> The rise of the Super Class ... is a seminal development in modern Britain, as critical as the rise of the gentry before the English Civil War and the rise of organized labour a century ago, and rivalled in contemporary significance only by the disintegration of the manual working class.[2]

As recently as 2006 it was argued that 'This has been a period of elite consolidation for which there is no parallel in the country's history';[3] that 'There is a certain swagger about the City of London these days';[4] and that – in relation to the global dimensions of this ascendancy – 'This new financial elite is the true heir to the imperial legacy' ... 'here is an elite of the elites whose power has grown to a dimension that is truly imperial in the modern world'.[5]

These elites have by no means been unseated by recent events, but things are not quite the same. There have been cracks in the self assurance. Can this moment of potential fracturing be seized upon to turn this from being a financial crisis into a wider political questioning that might shift the balance of social forces? For that to happen there need to be more than economic arguments.

THE 'NEOLIBERAL' SOCIAL SETTLEMENT

It is certainly the case that the socio-economic settlement of the past thirty years is broken. There has to be, at least, a readjustment. And this in itself opens up the political battlefield. The first elements of the economic structure that underpinned this settlement were, of course, set down under Thatcher – through the double move of the decimation of mining and manufacturing, especially in employment terms and with the social implications that go along with that, and the ascendancy of finance and its wide halo of surrounding sectors. That stage in the process was hugely contested – in defensive mode from the industrial and mining regions, and with proposals for an alternative way out of the crisis of the social-democratic settlement from the cities, chief among them London, where finance and the new elite had (and has) its seat of power. It was then, too, that began that shift in common sense towards neoliberal terms – the inevitability and rightness of market forces, the primacy of the sturdy competitive individual. It drew on longer-term cultural changes that had been under way since the 1960s to turn them into tools for capital and the right. It went down very well in the South and East of England, outside of London. But it was the bargain struck by New Labour that generalised this shift across the country into a full social settlement.[6] This bargain aimed to continue with the shape of the private-sector economy installed by Thatcher, with its prioritisation of and obeisance to the finance sector, and to use that sector to provide the tax surplus (or what remained of its potential yield after deductions through tax havens, non-dom status, an effectively regressive tax regime, and many pieces of imaginative accounting) to fund the social-democratic infrastructure.[7]

Everything depended on finance. It was to be the way out from the long decline of the British economy; it was to assert once again an imperial presence for that economy within the international division of labour; and it was to provide income to the exchequer for the expansion of public-sector investment and services. And voices from finance themselves put much work into promoting their role as the 'golden goose' of the nation. This was not, though, as it is often painted, just a question of backing a 'sector' of the economy; it was also the promotion of specific class interests.

This social settlement had effects that we know about well – the steep rise in 'inequality of the top', the growth of the new elite and a stratum of private-sector professionals, and many related developments (see notes 2, 3, 4 and 5 above). It also set off other social dynamics and produced or reinforced new social relationships. One such was the entrainment of the mass of people into financialisation. Through the practices of privatisation, of health, pensions, housing, people became entangled with the finance sector in ways which the financiers could harvest for 'investment' in SIVs, derivatives and assets. By this means millions of people became both materially enrolled into the interests of finance in the short term (even if structurally in the long term their interests would be elsewhere) and ideologically acculturated into its ways of thinking.

There were always weaknesses in this New Labour bargain. There was, for instance, the problem of employment. John Buchanan et al point to the way that publicly supported employment covered over the failure of the private sector to generate jobs.[8] It was a failure that was partly concealed by privatisation – which apparently added to private-sector employment levels – when in fact these were not new jobs but transfers, and were thus still directly dependent on state funding. The inherent precariousness of this model should have been evident.

Geographically, moreover, this was a social settlement that tore the nation apart.[9] The finance and associated sectors are overwhelmingly concentrated in (a small part of) London and the South East. The national geometries of power became even more focused on those regions; and the geography of the democratic deficit became even more glaring. Other regions became increasingly dependent on public-sector and para-state employment, nonetheless being drawn in to the new hegemony, of audit and market-thinking, by the changes introduced into those sectors themselves.[10] Within London, acute inequalities made the very social reproduction of the city impossible without special measures (key workers; a specifically *London* living wage, etc). The inequality in growth between regions resulted in differentials in house-price rises that further exacerbated national inequality. This was certainly not a geography that had been voted for.

Even before the crash, then, the frailties of this socio-economic strategy were apparent.

Moreover they were made more acute by the internal dynamics of the settlement. In particular, the prioritisation of finance led to a self-reinforcing dominance. There is a tree called the upas tree, beneath and around which nothing else can grow. It has been used as a meta-phor for regional and city economies that are dominated by a single sector that crowds out and/or stunts the growth of all others.[11] ('Crowding out' is usually a term used by those who would wish to prune back the public sector, but Buchanan et al argue that over the last two decades public-sector employment, far from crowding out growth in the private sector, has been compensating for its absence.) In the social settlement of the last thirty years in the UK, and as a structural consequence of this economic strategy, it has been finance and its associated sectors that have been the upas tree. The conflict between finance and industry is one with a long history in the UK, but it takes specific forms in different conjunctural moments. Over the last thirty years the dominance of finance has actively harmed the interests of other parts of the economy. At macro-level its dominant voice on exchange rates and its commitment to short-termism have been the problem; within London the effect on land and property prices, especially in the area around the City, and the advance buying-up of land and property, have threatened the diversity of the capital's economy; between regions a host of dynamics has been set in play, most particularly the draining from all other regions of professionally qualified workers into the maw of London and the South East. It is not, then, just that finance was prioritised for strategic regions, but that the dynamics of that very bargain increased the dominance of finance at the expense of other potential sources of growth.

And then it imploded.

AN ALLIANCE AGAINST THE DOMINANCE OF FINANCE: FOR A MORE BALANCED SOCIETY

The vortex of the current moment is the crisis in the financial sector, and the nature of the political response to it. (Indeed, insisting on this, rather than accepting the public-sector deficit as the crisis, is itself a central political task.) But, as argued above, the dominance by the financial sector was already a problem, even before that sector's implosion, and needed to be tackled on a much broader front. Finance and financial modes of calculation are emblematic of a wider mode of being, one that any left political strategy should be challenging. And there is also the question of democracy. The voice of the City is powerful in policy-making. The judgement of 'the markets' hangs over everything, setting the parameters within which political debate can operate. This assertion of economic power exposes the thinness of our political democracy. One central political priority must be to take advantage of this moment of relative weakness at the crux of this constellation and lever open those wider politics.

It is often pointed out that this crisis is different from the disloca- tion that brought the end of the post-war social-democratic settlement in that it was not made by the pressure of social forces or, directly, by social struggle. It was an implosion. There are in that sense no 'forces' at the ready. This is correct so far as it goes. But the social forces that produce a crisis are not necessarily the ones that will point to an alter- native way out. The forces that generated the crisis of the post-war social-democratic settlement tended, when the crisis came, to respond mainly in defence of the old settlement. There need also to be creative alternatives (in the 1980s some of these came, for example, from the urban left). In the present moment there are, contrary to what is often said, plenty of ideas and alternative political strategies. The problem is that these ideas do not have a social base, or purchase in the wider population. This problem for the left is compounded by the way in which so many of the radical challenges it made to the post-war hege- mony (feminism, the rejection of an undifferentiated 'public', the acknowledgement of heterogeneity, the stress on flexibility and flow rather than rigidity ...) have been in a thousand ways recuperated into the current hegemonic project, taken up in ways we never meant, turned to use as flexibilised labour, selfish individualism, and argu- ments against collectivism and the state. 'Liberation' turned into lifestyle capitalism. Cries of 'yes but ...' and 'we never meant that' do not have much political appeal. And so we find ourselves wrong- footed, and yet further disarmed.

This lack of voice was all too evident in the ease with which the financial crisis itself, a result of the structure of finance and of the actions of the super-rich, has been converted into a need for public- sector cuts. There is no need here to reiterate the 'illogicality' of this – that the poor are paying for the sins of the rich, that it was state intervention that saved the day, that much of the deficit results from the recession that followed the financial collapse, that such a strategy will curtail the possibility of growth, and likely plunge us more deeply into recession, etc, etc. The point to note for the moment is simply the astounding ease with which this re-narrativisation was achieved.

The question then arises as to what kinds of changes these cuts in public-sector expenditure will themselves bring about, and what kinds of defensive social forces might arise. At the sharpest end, undoubtedly, will be the ranks of public-sector workers, potentially in alliance with those who depend on their services. Most generally, Con-Lib policies will yet further sharpen economic inequality. Over the last thirty years the biggest statistical contribution to this widening inequality has come through growth in income and numbers at the rich end of the scale. With cutbacks in public expenditure – which will have impacts both on welfare and on jobs – this will change – the already poor are likely to be hit hardest. And there will be further differentiations. Whereas the prime producers of, and beneficiaries from, the disaster of the last thirty years have been very highly paid men, the cost of paying for the collapse of that period will, through public-expenditure cuts, be borne far more by women. Can these patent unfairnesses be the ground for finding new political voices?

And then there is geography. The North-South divide within the United Kingdom continued to widen under New Labour. Moreover the economic strategy of the last three decades changed the nature of that divide, dramatically reinforcing some inherited characteristics and introducing new ones, to form a new national spatial division of labour. There is the continuing centralisation of power into London and the South East (the North-South divide is about more than comparative levels of income and unemployment). There is the continuing loss of manufacturing employment. And, most of all, there is the fact that the social settlement of the last period has left some regions, outside of London and the South East, perilously dependent on the public sector for sources of employment as well as for welfare. In any serious programme of cuts in public expenditure they stand to be devastated. This is a regional inequality that, like the dominance of finance, has an internal dynamic that makes it self-reinforcing. The lack of voiced anger in the regions outside London and the South East is extraordinary. The official representatives of those regions have for too long acquiesced in the dominant narrative that no regional policy should in any way hold back London/the South East, and that the other regions must be regenerated by 'standing on their own feet' (while all the while London/the South East's problems of congestion and inflation are ameliorated by state intervention and subsidy). What has been problematical for the left in the past has been an understanding of this geography of inequality in terms of competition: the North *versus* the South. And so the poverty in London has been pitted, for political voice, against the poverty of the regions of the North and West. It is a problem that has frequently disfigured, and hampered, struggles on the left (for examples, see *World City*). Certainly these are poverties that are produced and experienced in different ways: in the context of acute inequality in London, in the dismal draining of hope in parts of the North and West. It is often remarked that the regional problem of the North and West is regeneration, while the regional problem of London/the South East is redistribution. But the two have the same sources, and it is time for an alliance across them, challenging the centrality and power of the City constellation in both the national economy and the national geography.

All of this is about a 'grassroots' response, based in trades unions, local alliances, feminist networks … and it is the strengthening of these voices that is right now most important. Unless and until that happens, the Labour Party seems unlikely to come out and redefine the political field. For that is what is needed.

However, none of these potential voices of protest will carry much weight without the ability to propose an alternative. And here we are in a vice, for in purely economic terms the grip of the financial sector and its wider constellation is real. In the years of its pomp finance worked hard to convince us that it was the golden goose upon which, in the end, all the rest depended.

To the extent that this was so it was by no means the result of untrammelled market forces; rather it grew out of political strategy, from Margaret Thatcher on, combined with the propaganda work put in by the sector and its representatives.

But it is important to understand that finance is *not* simply the golden goose. Over the last thirty years it has not been 'the motor of the economy' in the sense of driving investment. Its money went into assets; its result was redistribution. It was not a 'motor' in the sense of providing investment into other industries. (As many have pointed out, the undifferentiated language of 'investment' should here itself be challenged.) Indeed, as has been argued above, the dominance of finance has *weakened* other sectors, thereby reinforcing the fable of the golden goose.

But if there *is* a way in which finance is the golden goose it is as the provider of finances to the exchequer. Manufacturing, because of its much smaller size and lower profit rate, is very small by comparison in this regard.

However, manufacturing does still exist within the British economy. The UK is, by value, the sixth largest manufacturing economy in the world. Any way out of the current crisis, and especially one that avoids massive cuts in public expenditure, will need to generate growth. As Ha-Joon Chang has argued, that growth cannot come from the financial sector.[12] Much of it must come from non-financial sectors. This will be a hard road, but there are clear links here to the intersecting crises of climate change and oil-depletion, and the programme in the Green New Deal for a green army of workers to address, through new industries including recycling and repair, not only the economic but the environmental threats.[13] There are, moreover, other clear advantages (political as well as economic) to such a strategy. For one thing, an industrial strategy need not necessarily be very expensive – much can be achieved through regulations and incentives. The German commitment to environmentalism provided a framework, ideological as well as economic, within which green industries could flourish. Secondly, there is no reason why green industries should be so concentrated in London/the South East. Indeed, some of them by their nature will need to be located in relation to the distribution of the population. There could thus be a positive counter-dynamic to the currently increasing regional inequality. And, thirdly, an active industrial strategy (brilliantly argued for in Chang's paper on industrial policy, see note 12) would itself present an ideological challenge. As Chang pointed out in May, after decades of the free-market approach 'such an aversion to industrial policy has developed in Britain that there is hardly any debate on it in the current election campaign'.[14] One element of an alternative strategy must therefore be to argue for a rebalancing away from finance.

But the ideological challenge must also be wider than that – it will be crucial, as argued above, to reconnect and interweave the ideological and the economic. One central question is economic democracy. What happened to collectivity, to all those intimations of a return to cooperativism and mutualism that were around when the banks were first under attack; when the *principles* of economic organisation were also up for question? Again, one feels, much of the energy and imagination that might start to embed such ideas more widely will have to come from grassroots initiatives. Many of the political meetings I have been to since the elections have stressed the importance of 'bottom-up' organisation. Labour's performance in the 2010 local elections was certainly helped by their being held on the same day as national ones, but it was nonetheless in places impressive. It won control of Liverpool, Coventry, Doncaster, St Helens, Hartlepool, Oxford, and a host of London boroughs. There may be reasons to be depressed about the sharp geographical divides, but is there a basis here for a fightback led from local level? A new 'new urban left'?

Any effective strategy to reduce the dominance of finance over the rest of the economy will involve directly challenging its hegemonic stories: that it is the golden goose, that it is socially useful, or even economically useful in the sense of a productive economy; the constant threats to leave each time there is the most timid of challenges to their interests are null and void (they don't actually go, and it is a moot point whether we should care anyway).

What is at issue here is directly taking on class interests. It means defining enemies; it means delineating political frontiers. And this is something Labour has persistently refused to do. The Green New Deal has begun the task of identifying the groups that might be recruited to such a cause, writing of:

> an exciting possibility of a new political alliance: an alliance between the labour movement and the green movement, between those engaged in manufacturing and the public sector, between civil society and academia, industry, agriculture and those working productively in the service industries (p6).

'Such a political alliance', it argues, 'is vital if we are to challenge the dominance of the finance sector in the economy, its threat to the productive sectors of the economy, its corruption of the political system, and its corrosion of social and environmental values' (p6). Quite so. It is important to note that these groups – potential political voices – do not 'show up' as classes. As Stuart Hall argued in Chapter 4:

> That's not because class is unimportant or has disappeared ... But when you look at the theatre of politics, classes don't appear in their already-united form. Unifying into a 'historical bloc' is part of what politics does.[15]

This also means that formulations of a simple choice between working class and middle class, or about 'moving to the centre' or not, as though it were a smooth spectrum, rest on an inadequate imaginary. What is really at issue is identifying, and taking the lead in formulating and articulating, real – and complex and multifarious – interests and attitudes on the ground.

Such an alliance could be international too, and this not only in the sense of alliances with those in other countries facing common threats, but also in recognition of the new imperial role of the City of London as a key node in the generation of the ideology, and the form of finance, that led to these problems in the first place.[16] With such potential allies, taking on the burgeoning strata of the super rich and the interests of finance and its surrounding sectors should not be impossible.

WHAT DOES NEOLIBERAL HEGEMONY REPRESENT?

And yet, what has also to be addressed is the astonishing success of the ideological hegemony of the last thirty years. It is this that lies behind the supreme ease with which the re-narrativisation was achieved: that while 'they' caused the problem it is 'we', through public-sector cuts, who must pay. In part, this hegemony raises political issues about the current state of democratic debate in the UK, and in particular about the role of the media: the question of media ownership and influence is absolutely central. It is also a hegemony in part established through the enrolment of people's material interests, most obviously through the privatisation of pensions. But it is also more than these things.

There is (was?) an amazing fit between the characteristics of finance and the wider feel of society. Finance's nature of pure exchange, its apparent (only apparent) disembeddedness, its prioritisation of flow over territory, of movement over stability, its (again only apparent) non-materiality, the individual(istic) character of its 'production process'. All of this chimed somehow with the spirit of the times. Jürgen Kädtler has written of financial rationality being a power in itself;[17] it was also a form of rationality that became generalised to – or perhaps was the most precise expression of relations in – wider society.

The public bail-out of the banks led to talk of the end of neoliberalism. We know now – at policy level – it is not so. But more importantly, in popular discourse there is a lot left of neoliberalism. There is a profound embedded resignation to the naturalness of market forces. There is a pervasive negativity towards the state, reinforced by things like the politics of spectacle around MPs' expenses. These things are deep within popular discourse, even if often contradictorily so.

All of which leads to a final point that has often been obscured in the debates about neoliberalism. 'Neoliberalism' as a purely economic doctrine – a doctrine about how to run an economy – was always (if not only then certainly in part) a tool in the armoury of a battle between social forces: the battle to restore profits at the end of the social-democratic settlement against a labour force that had made substantial gains. Its hegemony rests in part on the ability to hold together contradictory practices in an over-arching narrative. Of course, much of neoliberalism chimes politically with elements of a classic right-wing agenda. But its nostrums have always, even in its pomp, been drawn on selectively – used when useful but totally disregarded when not. In that sense, mobilising the state to bail out the banks was not an anomaly. It was more blatant, more obvious, more crucial, and in that sense ideologically and politically more important. But it was not new. And this highlights a disjunction between the legitimating hegemonic ideology on the one hand and actual economic/political practice on the other. And what this in turn indicates is that at bottom what is at issue here, or what will be at issue if we are going to turn this into a real ruptural moment, is a submerged contest over the balance of social forces. For it would be possible to defeat 'neoliberalism' and still to lose the social struggle. The same class forces could remain in power.

NOTES

1. For more on conjunctural analysis see S. Hall and D. Massey, 'Interpreting the crisis', Chapter 4.
2. A. Adonis and S. Pollard, *A class act: the myth of Britain's classless society*, Penguin 1998.
3. H. Williams, *Britain's power elites: the rebirth of a ruling class*, Constable 2006.
4. M. Dickson, 'London: capital gain', *Financial Times*, 27.3.06 (report on *The New City*).
5. H. Williams, 'How the City of London came to power', *Financial Times*, 21.3.06, p15.
6. See P. Devine, 'The 1970s and after: the political economy of inflation

and the crisis of social democracy', *Soundings* 32, spring 2006; D. Massey, *World City*, Polity 2007; S. Hall, 'New Labour's double-shuffle', *Soundings* 24, autumn 2003.

7. 'Finance' throughout is shorthand for finance and its surrounding sectors.
8. J. Buchanan, J. Froud, S. Johal, A. Leaver and K. Williams, 'Undisclosed and unsustainable: problems of the UK national business model', CRESC Working Paper Series 75, Manchester University and Open University 2009.
9. See Massey, *World City*.
10. See Hall, 'New Labour's double-shuffle'.
11. S. Checkland, *The upas tree: Glasgow 1875-1975: a study in growth and contraction*, Glasgow University Press 1976.
12. H-J. Chang, 'Industrial policy: can we go beyond an unproductive confrontation?' mimeo, presented at Annual World Bank Conference on Development Economics, June 2009, and New Political Economy Group, April 2010; and 'UK needs a selective industrial policy', *Guardian comment is free*, 3.5.10.
13. nef, *A Green New Deal*, nef 2008.
14. Chang, 'UK needs a selective industrial policy'.
15. Hall and Massey, 'Interpreting the crisis', Chapter 4, p.66.
16. D. Massey, 'London inside-out', *Soundings* 32, spring 2006.
17. J. Kädtler, 'Financialisation or: bargaining on economic rationalities', paper presented to CRESC Conference, *Finance in question/Finance in crisis*, Manchester, April 2010.

6. THE CRISIS OF A SOCIAL SYSTEM

Michael Rustin

Is the current political settlement sustainable?

The persuasive view that Stuart Hall set out in Chapter 1 is that the Coalition is the most radical government since Thatcher. He describes its ferocious programme to further subjugate Britain to the hegemony of neoliberalism as an ideology and world-view. Doreen Massey's complementary argument is that resistance to these conservative forces has to be mounted from outside the compromised perspectives of social democracy with its half-hearted qualifications to market-led regimes whose domination it largely accepts as necessary and inevitable. She argues for a politics based on alternative values and on forms of agency whose potential comes in part from outside the conventional political system.

Both of these arguments, most of which I agree with, are organised around a dynamic conception of ideology, which after all is what 'neoliberalism' essentially is. In Hall's chapter the concept of ideology, however, becomes expanded, such that the term 'neoliberalism' is not merely employed to describe a doctrine or system of ideas, but becomes a description of an entire social formation, seen as the enactment of its animating ideological principles. One can say, without disparagement, that this is a kind of 'culturalist' approach to political analysis. Since neoliberal ideology is indeed the organising principle of the great transformation of our times, this perspective captures much of what needs to be understood about the 'present conjuncture'.

A SYSTEMIC CRISIS

Nevertheless, I want to frame my contribution to this debate in slightly different terms. Suppose we think in terms of the development not of an ideological system, but of a social system, whose dominant ideas and mentalities are only one of its components. Suppose one reverts to the antiquated term capitalism, as the name not merely of an ideology but of an ensemble of interrelated elements (modes of production, distribution, social control, socialisation, communication, military power, etc). Suppose one further reintroduces into this model the idea of social classes, in all their complex aspects, and identifies these rather than the ideologies that both construct them and are constructed by them as the prime agencies of change. Any conceptual framing of these issues has its own problems, as arguments within Marxist social theory over recent decades have taught us. Nevertheless, some light might be thrown on our situation through the use of a 'social system discourse' which an ideology-focused account may not provide.

The question which this other framing of the issues may enable us to ask concerns the stability and viability of the systems animated by neoliberal ideology. 'Systems theories', in both their sociological and structuralist Marxist variants, were always concerned with the precon- ditions of social equilibrium (the issue for functionalism) or potential disequilibrium (the issue for Marxists such as Althusser). The question I want to raise concerns the 'equilibrium' or otherwise of one particular system, namely that of the United Kingdom's national version of capi- talism, shaped as it has been by its own specific history. How stable, now, is this particular configuration? My purpose is not to critique in normative terms the neoliberal project for Britain, but rather to ask what its outcomes are likely to be, here in Britain. As a governmental project, can it work, even in its own terms? And should it fail, in what forms might failure manifest itself, and what opportunities might this failure offer to the development of alternative kinds of politics?[1]

It is certainly the case that global capitalism has been enjoying a spectacular advance over the past thirty years. This advance began first with the economic and political crisis of the 1970s in the West, and the victory of neoliberals in the struggles of that period. Its second major precondition was the collapse of European Communism, and the emergence of China as a new kind of hybrid formation, capitalist in its economy but still with a notionally Communist one-party form of government. The regime described by Hall and Massey stands as the local British instantiation of this world-wide advance of capitalism. Its strategies have been at some points in the vanguard of this develop- ment (for example in the social technology of privatisation which was exported to the world from Thatcherite Britain, and in the 'big bang' of the deregulation of the financial sector in 1985); while in other respects they have taken the form of more reactive and defensive responses to the competitive pressures of this encroaching system, for example in the deflation of the 1980s, and perhaps in the current excesses of deficit reduction.

We can perhaps now understand the post-second world war moment in which the aspirations of the generation of those now over fifty or so were formed as the aberration, and the sway of capital, markets, and the ideology of individualism which now prevails as closer to the historical norm. It was once inviting to interpret the emergence of social democracy as the culmination of an evolutionary process, in which aspirations grew in harmony with material and political possibilities. T.H. Marshall's influential account described a historical development in which first civil rights, then political rights, and then economic and social rights had been successfully claimed by means of sustained democratic pressure exercised by the people upon first aristocratic then bourgeois elites.[2] Raymond Williams' *The Long Revolution* added the dimension of cultural struggle and emancipation to this description, while already warning against the visible capture of democratic agencies by the authoritarian structures which they were supposedly seeking to transform.[3] This narrative in effect reformulated an existing Whig view of British history as the evolution of liberalism in more popular social democratic terms. It corresponded, as the earlier Whig view had done, to a particular historical moment in which the particular configuration of class forces whose view it embodied had arrived, if not at the summit of power, at least somewhere within view of the summit. As Marx wrote: 'Mankind thus inevitably sets itself only such tasks as it is able to solve, since closer examination will always show that the problem itself arises only when the material conditions for its solution are already present or at least in the course of formation'.[4] The post-war years were certainly the period in which a self-conscious and substantially organised working class in Britain had come to form a numerically larger part of the population than ever before. In this period, governments across western Europe and North America were active in managing systems which saw a significant rise in social protection, welfare provision, employee power, and managed political compromises between contending social classes.

It is now evident that the equilibria established both in the welfare states of Europe, and to a lesser degree in the USA, and in the balance of power between western capitalism and state socialism in the east, were only temporary, the latter even more spectacularly so than the former. The significance of state socialism in this configuration was primarily as a countervailing threat, rather than as an appealing alternative to democratic capitalism, but as such it constrained the western democracies of both centre-right and centre-left varieties to concede social rights and protections to their peoples, in order to win and retain support from them for parliamentary systems of government, and for the market economies over which they presided. Both these equilibria of forces were the products of a particular crisis – the rise of Nazism and Fascism – and the eventual collective and democratic response to it. It was the defeat of Fascism which led to the advance of social democracy across western Europe, as well as the imposition of the state socialist system upon eastern Europe. Another important element in this post-war reconfiguration of power was the impetus to collective solidarity and organisation that came from the material and social technology of industrial production.

The welfare settlement in Britain and the USA exploded in social conflict in the 1970s, which ended in the victories of neo-conservativism under Reagan, Thatcher and their successors. This brought about a major rebalancing of power. Deregulation and globalisation have proved to be potent means of advancing the power of capital over the political and social forces which had set limits to it. The global organisation of markets has become a more effective form of power than colonial domination by military force, which towards the end of the era of empires was demanding large expenditures of resources and blood, though with lessening economic or other benefit to the imperial metropolises. The bond markets, multinational corporations and the IMF, and indeed the 'soft power' represented by the global diffusion of mass consumption, have mostly proved capable of deploying power more effectively and efficiently than gunboats and armies (though across the Middle East, where the key resource of oil is at stake, military imperialism persists, with its unavailing quest to build capitalist states through the use of armed force).

As Meghnad Desai has reminded us, Marx has proved to be correct in his prediction that capitalism would continue its advance until it had subsumed the entire world under its dominion.[5] It is important that we should see the condition of capitalism in Britain in this larger global context. In the remainder of this chapter I shall be considering how limited is the scope for manoeuvre that now seems to be available to British governments.

THE BRITISH CASE

Hall and Massey each emphasise the radical ambition of the neoliberal project in its British incarnation. They see this as it is embodied in the programmes of the current Coalition, in those of its Thatcherite predecessor, and in New Labour's abject surrender to the values and pressures of neoliberalism in during its thirteen years of office. I, by contrast, will draw attention to the fragility of this neoliberal project in Britain, and to the unlikelihood that it can succeed in achieving the stable hegemony it aims for. It is certainly the case that the Coalition project is exceptionally bold, and that in their broad ambitions if not in their grasp of details the Cameron Conservatives were well prepared to make the most of their arrival in government. But the Coalition's aims also carry with them, almost as the necessary concomitant of their radicalism, a high risk of failure. One can see the Tory-led Coalition government, as no doubt do some of its members, as determined to render irreversible the imposition of the power of capital and markets over all the democratic and collective forces which have over many decades resisted their domination. But one can also view its programme as an ideologically driven attempt to resolve the deep crisis faced by the United Kingdom in the context of the global market system, which in reality has little hope of success.

This brings us back to analysis of the present conjuncture, a theme which *Soundings* has been pursuing over the last two years or so.[6] In these discussions we drew attention to similarities between the present situation and the period of crisis of the 1970s, which was so presciently described in *Policing the Crisis* by Hall and his co-authors in 1979. The chief parallel lies in the inescapable weight of problems to which no solution can be found within the existing framework of ideas and capabilities. During the 1970s, as Hall reminds us, insurgencies of various kinds threatened the governmental and economic system in Britain with virtual collapse. The administrations of Wilson, Heath and Callaghan succeeded one another in rapid succession because of their recurrent failures to resolve the situation. Inflation, strike action, nationalist pressures from Scotland and Northern Ireland, and new axes of social and cultural conflict, were indicators of the depth of the impasse. As had been the case in the great crisis of pre-first world war Britain, working-class militancy was the most dynamic force in a many-faceted insurgency against established structures. But what ensued from these conflicts was a political deadlock within a state of apparent chaos, rather than the transformative process of democratisation which rising aspirations of many kinds had inchoately put on to the agenda. Thatcherism did indeed provide a 'counter-revolutionary' alternative of a kind to a failing social and political settlement. The Thatcherites certainly had a clear understanding that their priority was to achieve a decisive defeat of what they saw as a collectivist threat to both markets and social hierarchy. This was, for the right at least, an explicit form of class warfare.

Hall's suggestion is that this solution has, as it were, come around again. Only perhaps this time with the capacity to achieve a decisive resolution of the British crisis in favour of a fully-dominant neoliberalism. But one can interpret this situation differently, in systemic terms. The implosion of the credit crunch has revealed that the apparently continuous prosperity which the UK seemed to have enjoyed, from the post-Black Wednesday years of the previous Tory government to the end of the 'no more boom and bust' years of Brown, was partially an illusion. Britain has been living out the false prosperity of two speculative bubbles, those of house price inflation, and of an unfounded asset boom. Real incomes for the majority have remained largely stagnant over this entire period, as they have even more in the United States. The falling costs of many commodities, due to their production in emerging low-wage economies, and advances in technology (e.g. IT) have, however, led to some rise in consumption in real-value terms.

The Coalition's dominant idea (much more important to it than its 'Big Society') is that the core problem of the British economy has been excessive public spending. Its particular critique is of the alleged excesses of the past ten years, but the implication of its analysis is that the problem is much longer-lasting. Ostensibly and immediately, the problem is to reduce the public deficit, as a defensive operation to protect Britain from the (extremely unlikely) threat of sovereign debt default. But its longer-term purpose is more fundamental: the explicit aim of Coalition economic strategy is radically to alter the balance between private and state expenditures in the British economy.

What grounds are there for believing that a viable model for economic success, and thus of system stability, in the UK can be based on emulating the example of the USA? What leading economic sectors and what dormant entrepreneurial capacities does the UK harbour that could enable Britain to manifest an American-style dynamism, once the alleged shackles of high taxation, excessive regulation, and the 'crowding out' by public of private investment, are removed? This is an especially pertinent question given that the American economic model is itself in severe difficulties, and in Britain the best-rewarded and most attractive occupations for ambitious entrants to the labour market for two decades have been not industry but financial services and their associated professions. It is becoming clear that the excesses of the Coalition's deficit reduction programme will slow if not abort the economy's recovery from the credit crunch. But more important even than this is the probability that its implicit economic strategy, a repetition of the Thatcherite 'scorched earth' programme of the 1980s but without its cushion of newly-discovered North Sea oil, will fail. It will prove to be a wager on growth through entrepreneurship that will fail to appear in anything like the scale required. Joseph Stiglitz has argued that the dominant neoliberal approach to the post-crisis situation (of which the Coalition's is but one extreme variant) is flawed, in so far as its downward pressure on employee incomes and social protection merely leads to a state of 'underconsumption' in which few enterprises can grow. Neoliberal ideology has an additional role in this situation over and above that described above by Hall and Massey. In their articles they rightly argue that it rationalises the remaking of an entire social system in the light of its world-view. But it is also specifically 'ideological' in its misrepresentation of what is feasible and attainable through following its prescriptions. For Britain, it is the route to another economic train-crash.

THE POLITICS OF THE COALITION

What are the politics of this critical situation? How probable is it that the Coalition will deliver a sufficient economic recovery in four years time to win the further victory for its allied Parties, or for the Conservatives alone, to underpin a neoliberal hegemony for the long-term?

It is becoming evident that the Lib Dems made a major tactical error in joining the Cameron government on the terms they did. By accepting a version of the 'deficit problem' that Vince Cable had opposed during the election campaign, the Lib Dems undermined their own credibility, and rendered themselves powerless to contest Tory economic strategy. They seemed to forget that the Tories had failed to win the general election, and that the actual balance of public opinion revealed by the election result was, if one took into account the support for Labour, closer to their own centrist position than to that of the Tories. Only the achievement of electoral reform, even in the weak form of the alternative vote, would have made this arrangement to their advantage, and they were outmanoeuvred on this too.

Until now, the Lib Dems have been trapped by their partners in government. They have been (and still are) at risk of electoral annihilation if the Tories were to declare the Coalition unworkable and demand an election. Having started down the road of compliance, it is difficult for the Lib Dems to depart from it. It has been a remarkable political achievement by Cameron to have achieved this position of domination from the starting point of a partial electoral failure.

But it must be remembered that popular support for the radical Tory project is far from solid. Indeed the Tories are having to make such heavy use of the partially synthetic deficit crisis (while having little to offer on the real economy) for just this reason. The Coalition has acknowledged that the first few years of the government will be difficult. But when the electoral costs of public expenditure cuts and economic contraction begin to affect Tory as well as Lib Dem support, the balance of power in the Coalition may change, and the Lib Dems could regain some autonomy. Indeed they need to do so, to give themselves a chance in the next election.

Lib Dem dissent over the NHS reforms (initiated by Shirley Williams) may be the beginning of a reconnection with that crucial element of the Lib Dems' electoral base which values public services. If opinion moves against the Coalition's neoliberalism (as it eventually did against the Tory governments of the 1990s), the Lib Dems may rediscover this submerged part of their identity. Historical changes in class alignments in Britain are a later theme of this chapter, and transformations in the Liberal (and now Lib Dem) parties have often been a significant indicator of these.

It is unlikely that the Tories will be able to deliver a credible form of economic recovery, sufficient to give legitimacy to their dismantling of public services and their erosion of public goods. It is because the majority of British citizens, at existing levels of income, cannot afford self-provision in the spheres of social care, education and health, that universal public services remain in demand, and this is why Labour won support for improving them. There is also an attachment to good public provision in other spheres (the popularity of the BBC, the enjoyment of public space, widespread interest in conservation), which makes the ultra-individualist agenda of the neoliberals hard to impose on Britain.

It is quite possible therefore that the Coalition's neoliberal plan to resolve the British crisis will fail, and that we will find ourselves within four years with a Labour government or a Labour-Lib Dem coalition – however, one struggling with the same intractable economic problems as those faced by the present Coalition. The major problem may not be how to bring this political outcome about: from Labour's present position, which is by no means as bad as might have been feared two years ago, it may take only reasonable political competence to bring off. The larger problem may be how to convert a positive electoral outcome into an engagement with the problems of British society that transcends the softened and moderated form of neoliberalism which was all New Labour could achieve. A Labour or Labour Lib-Dem programme which merely rows back from the more radical elements of the Coalition will not suffice, as Hall and Massey also argue. Furthermore, looking ahead, another governmental failure to resolve these problems would be dangerous, perhaps opening the way to an irruption from the populist right such as we have seen elsewhere in Europe when decline threatens.

CHANGING CLASS STRUCTURES IN BRITAIN

In the early 1960s, a debate took place about the failure of what (even then!) was called 'modernisation' in Britain. It was argued that Britain was still unduly oriented towards what remained of its empire, and that its economic development was held back by this priority. A number of economists criticised the overvaluation of sterling, which they held was a consequence of privileging the financial over the industrial sectors of the economy. Excessive expenditures on defence were understood in related terms. The continued power of aristocracy and its networks of patronage, which were deeply entangled in finance and rent-based wealth, were also viewed as obstacles to progress. The most intellectually substantial version of this critique was developed by Perry Anderson, who argued that Britain had failed to achieve an authentic bourgeois revolution of the kind that had occurred in revolutionary France.[7] As leaders of thoroughly middle-class origin began to take control of both Tory and Labour parties (Wilson, Heath, Thatcher, Callaghan), and as 'modernisation' in its various meanings became the dominant motif of successive governments, it might have seemed that this debate had been resolved, in a final triumph of bourgeois norms and mentalities. But such an assumption would be mistaken. Transformations in the order of class and status in Britain have indeed taken place over this half-century, but much in the old order of property, privilege and hierarchy has remained intact.

The critique of the excessive role of banking and finance in the British economy has even more relevance after the credit crunch. Wilson's 'technological revolution' scarcely happened, and what was left of the manufacturing industry which it was intended to modernise was decimated by the deliberately deflationary policies of the 1980s. The ultra-bourgeois Thatcher presided over an economic strategy whose outcome was an even greater domination of the economy by the financial and banking sector than had existed before. The 'windfall' of North Sea oil had the distorting effects on the economy that 'free' mineral resources of this kind often do, making possible the neglect by elites of forms of wealth creation that depend on social co-operation, rather than on a kind of rent. The social relations of oil-rich states are rarely models to be emulated, and Britain has proved no exception.

Will Hutton developed a powerful argument in the 1990s which connected the under-performance of Britain's economy to its systems of governance.[8] Essentially this was a critique of irresponsible power – of shareholders prioritising short-term financial returns over long-term development, and of a system of corporate ownership which excluded most 'stakeholders' from a significant role in corporate governance. Indeed this pattern of ownership and control ensures that the relations between labour and capital remain largely antagonistic. Hutton's argument was linked to Charter 88's critique of the UK's constitution, which pointed to the privileges of birth and property that denied democratic voice and entitlement to the people. Arbitrary power was thus held to be the dysfunctional essence of governance in both the economic and political spheres.

The UK's continued involvement over this entire period in quasi-imperial military missions is a further indication of how little has changed in terms of its overseas orientation. The 'special relationship' with the United States has always been Britain's means of continuing its imperial role as a protected junior partner, once its own pre-eminence had ended.

What has, however, declined even further is the UK's capacity to steer its own economic development. National assertion becomes a mirage when the main arbiters of economic policy have become the global bond market. The state the British economy needs is not a weak state, nor merely a welfare state, but an enabling state, which has the capacity to sustain investment in the long term, and of promoting sustainable models of well-being. The social democratic division of labour which assigns to the state the role of (collective) consumer, and to private capital that of producer, is dysfunctional. Private capital in Britain cannot produce (and has therefore been gifted parts of the public sector in compensation), and the banks will not lend. There is still an urgent need for a new model for British capitalism.

How is it that, despite the many social changes which have taken place in Britain since the 1950s – for example the lessening in superficial distinctions of status – so much of its essential social structure and value-system remains the same? We can understand this more easily if we revisit the 'double shuffle' argument which Hall memorably deployed to characterise New Labour's politics of ambiguity – its justifying of the ways of capital to its property-less voters.[9] The double shuffle argument can be reformulated to refer to a wider strategy of class rule. Thus the ultra-bourgeois figure of Thatcher not only advanced the values of entrepreneurialism and markets, but also restored the authority of the state and the values of nationalism and empire. Dominant elites have learned to simulate more democratic and classless forms, while giving up little of their real power. The 'genius' of Blair (and of his style-follower Cameron) is precisely to seem 'ordinary' and 'modern', even while their commitment is to the preservation of the established order of property and privilege. Over the last thirty years, bourgeois and aristocratic modes of domination have further intertwined with one another, while the countervailing values of equality, democracy and citizenship have been weakened, as their base in working-class solidarity and collective sentiment has eroded. Not only this, but the 'working class' has become redefined as mere losers – to be morally improved and fitted to compete in the Great Market Society, culturally disrespected and humiliated (the 'chav' discourse), and socially cleansed from 'respectable' neighbourhoods. This is a move back from a society of class to a society of rank.[10] Social evolution in reverse.

Another way of putting it is to say that, historically, the rising bourgeoisie invariably faced a choice of how far to ally itself with the ordinary people, the large mass of the propertyless or working class, and how far with the previously established propertied elites, embedded as these are in the great institutions of the state. Whether states became democratic or authoritarian during the last two centuries was largely determined by how these alliances were made. (In Prussia, Austria and Russia in the late nineteenth century, the ancien regime effectively co-opted the bourgeoisie, but where bourgeois-working-class alliances secured power, parliamentary democracies were the outcome.[11]) In Britain a bourgeois-working-class alliance was instrumental in bringing about parliamentary democracy, with subsequent concessions of economic and social rights to the working class. But the bourgeoisie has always faced both ways. Although aristocracy per se might seem to have disappeared as a force from the British scene, and Thatcherism to have been a wholly bourgeois formation with neoliberalism as its ideology, the reality was always more complex. Norms of hierarchy and inheritance, and imperial and authoritarian attributes of the state, have continued throughout to exercise a shaping influence on British society, and are the legacies of aristocratic domination.

The past thirty years in Britain have seen a regressive development, in which assumptions of privilege and social closure that once seemed to be on the way out have subtly reasserted themselves. The cult of the super-rich, the co-option even of public sector managers into their ranks, the dispersal of the urban poor through housing and benefit policy, the culture of supposed 'excellence' and exclusivity in the university system, the immunity of the banks from retribution for their irresponsibility – all are indicators of this reassertion of the principle of hierarchy. Aristocratic and bourgeois forms of life and of domination appear to have dissolved into one another. Since education in modern technological societies has become a critical resource for the maintenance of wealth and privilege, money and political power are deployed to control access to it, through the public schools and their privileged access to leading universities – and at subaltern levels of the class structure through the covert reintroduction of educational selection. Because the media have become a crucial modern technology of power, its resources and skills must therefore be mastered by dominant elites. David Cameron is emblematic of this social development, an Etonian background having again become, half a century after Alec Douglas Home, an acceptable qualification for national leadership; while Cameron's previous career in public relations helped hone the skills which have become another essential resource in the establishment's repertoire. There is even, it must be said, a kind of dynamism in this development, for example in the monarchy 'modernising' itself through the marriage of Prince William to the graduate daughter of a modern entrepreneurial family (and perhaps leaping over the antediluvian figure of Prince Charles in the process). Governmental insistence on its commitment to social mobility and equal opportunity merely distracts attention (and is even a mechanism of unconscious denial) from the larger systemic processes which are making hierarchies steeper and opportunities more restricted. In this context we should note that the heirs of the Liberal Party in Britain – in the nineteenth century the party of the rising middle class, and frequently having played a progressive role in British politics – at the moment have moved closer to the Tory Party, traditionally the representative of old privilege. While the 1940s 'social liberalism' of Beveridge and Keynes articulated the logic of an inclusive class alliance under the aegis of progressive government, the individualist, anti-statist approaches of the Orange Book Liberals reject collectivism, returning to an alliance with the rentier class whose euthanasia Keynes once called for. But these alliances may not be set in stone.

Over several decades a complex process of social regression has been taking place, even as the ideology of liberalism has appeared to be dominant. In some spheres this was restrained by New Labour, in others it was accelerated. However, the British model of capitalism – democratic or otherwise – remains a failing one. The Coalition now offers an improbable remedy – an even fuller embrace of the market ideology that has brought the country to its present crisis. My argument is that a settlement of this kind is unlikely to be sustainable. The challenge for the left is to develop an analysis which can imagine an alternative pathway for development, in its many necessary dimensions. Nothing less than a renaissance of progressive political thinking, in its broadest dimensions, is now required.

NOTES

1. David Lockwood, linking Marxist and functionalist ideas, differentiated 'social integration' (determined by the existence of consensus or conflict) and 'system integration' (determined by whether a social structure experiences 'objective' contradictions). In Britain, while social integration remains strong, with limited institutional or ideological challenges to it, 'system integration' is much more uncertain, given pressures on employment and living standards. D. Lockwood, 'Social Integration and System Integration', in G.K. Zollschan and W. Hirsch (eds), *Explorations in Social Change*, Routledge and Kegan Paul 1964. See also my chapter, 'Reflections on the Present', in this volume.

2. T.H. Marshall, 'Citizenship and Social Class', in *Sociology at the Crossroads and other Essays*, Heinemann 1963.

3. R. Williams, *The Long Revolution*, Chatto and Windus 1961.

4. K. Marx, *Preface to The Critique of Political Economy*, 1859.

5. M. Desai, *Marx's Revenge: the Resurgence of Capitalism and the Death of Statist Socialism*, Verso 2002.

6. See 'Reflections on the Present' (see note 1); and S. Hall and D. Massey, 'Interpreting the Crisis', Chapter 4.

7. P. Anderson, 'Origins of the Present Crisis', *New Left Review*, 1/23 January-February 1964.

8. W. Hutton, *The State We're In*, Jonathan Cape 1995.

9. S. Hall, 'New Labour's Double-Shuffle', *Soundings* 24, 2003.

10. R. Williams, *Keywords: a Vocabulary of Culture and Society*, Fontana 1976.

11. W. Barrington Moore, *Social Origins of Dictatorship and Democracy*, Penguin 1966.

7. IDEOLOGY AND ECONOMICS IN THE PRESENT MOMENT

Doreen Massey

As I understand it, the conjunctural analysis we have discussed in *Soundings* is about deep structural movements.[1] It is not particularly about parliament and parties, though actions and events there may well be the spark that sets off tectonic shifts. A conjunctural approach leads us to examine the movements of the different instances in a social formation, and the potential social forces. The question that arises from this for the left is: is there going to be, and how can we contribute to the provocation of, a moment of rupture in which the different instances interlock in crisis and open up the ground for a shift in the balance of social power.

In terms of this architectonics of the conjuncture, the prime characteristic (in the sense especially of being the most debilitating for the left) is that we face a continuing economic crisis in the UK, but, as I shall go on to explore, although there are openings, there is no real crisis in the ideological formation that is described by Stuart Hall in Chapter 1. There has therefore been no significant shift in the balance of social forces (if anything it has shifted towards the elite strata). There has been no fracturing of the hegemonic common sense (if anything this too has shifted rightwards). Moreover, it is argued in what follows, without a serious engagement with the current ideological hegemony it will be impossible to break the stranglehold of the present economic discourse.

THE IDEOLOGICAL SCAFFOLDING

In this chapter I want to focus on the ideological thread in this structure. And I want to do so for two reasons: firstly that it does seem, as I shall argue, that there is here some real room for effective contestation; and secondly that there seems to be in this crisis a quite particular and complex intersection between the economic and the ideological that both is interesting in its own right and may offer openings for productive political engagement.

First, then, there *was* a moment at the height of the financial implosion when questions were raised that went far deeper than the economic. They went beyond the fact that the basic tenets of neoliberalism had been found wanting. They went beyond hostility to individual bankers – to touch upon, and question, the philosophy of greed and self-interest that underpinned their wealth and our crisis. There was not just a hostility to bonuses and such but a felt antipathy to the very mode of being human that had led us to this pass. Questions were raised of the wider ideological framing of life, and questions of ethics too. There were for a moment glimmerings of the possibility that the ideological underpinnings of the economic itself might be brought into the light and acknowledged.

Within months this sudden clarity seemed to have been obscured. Although it was widely agreed that in purely economic terms we could not return to 'business as usual' (although in fact it seems likely that broadly speaking we will), in ideological terms it was soon very much business as usual. Those bigger questions were buried – they ceased to be questions, and discussion was reabsorbed into the old common sense.

My own response (and I think that of others) to this disappearing act (and to the transformation of subsidiary issues – how did a crisis of banking turn into a crisis of government overspending?) was a kind of startled 'how did *that* happen?'. But of course it didn't just 'happen', the ideological ground had been prepared over years. The right, defined very broadly, had put in a huge amount of work. The discourse of the naturalness of market forces had long been won (see below). There had been a sustained attack on public-sector workers (on their wages, their pensions, their supposed job security ...). There was of course then no party-political opposition. Labour was unable to respond because it was itself implicated – though all too rarely do we hear it pointed out that the Tories were enthusiastic supporters of the main pillars of the system in which Labour had enmeshed itself – the general obeisance to finance, the refusal to regulate it seriously, and so forth. The complicity of Labour is often remarked upon, but the real problem – and the effect of its complicity in conjunctural terms – went far beyond the usually noted support for finance. New Labour subscribed totally to TINA – that there is no better way to do things, that we must resign ourselves. They reduced politics to administration ('what matters is what works', and so forth). And as a result they utterly failed to define political frontiers. This runs far deeper than implication through the selection of particular policies. It is about the very scaffolding of our political imaginations. And the vast bulk of the media has utterly bought into this too. It is not seriously open to deeper questioning or to alternative voices from the left. Indeed, the ownership and structure of the media should be a far higher priority for the left in political debate. Their impact has been enormous both in general (their near universal acquiescence in the 'cuts are necessary' position) and in particular campaigns (the MPs' expenses scandal was important in deflecting attention from the banks, for instance). In other words, the obscuring of the ideological issues momentarily laid bare by the financial crisis didn't just happen – it was a political result.

So the moment of possibility for ideological challenge seemed to pass. Perhaps, we thought, they had managed to suture it all together again. Or perhaps not; for there seem to be deeper shifts at work that evidence longer lasting unease. Even the political parties and those around them seem to recognise this. There is the discussion in Labour-oriented circles of the Good Society. There is Glasman and co's attempt to articulate something that has been called Blue Labour. There is all the happiness stuff. Further right there is Philip Blond and Jesse Norman. Even Cameron's Big Society, though it may be a cover for cuts (it *is*), is nonetheless crafted in a way that aims to touch on people's sense of aridity and depersonalisation (which the Tories attribute to the state, though it is far more characteristic of a market philosophy that sees us as preconstituted individuals who interact only through monetised exchange). Cameron muses that there is more to life than GDP ...

However inadequate the analyses and proposals offered up from some of these quarters (of which, more later), what their very existence may evidence is intimations that all is not well with the current ideological hegemony. There is an unease. The moment for an ideological challenge would seem still to be open.

The second reason for engaging here specifically with the ideological field is that the form of intersection of the economic and the ideological is quite particular to this conjunctural moment. There are a number of aspects to this.

To begin with, one of the most striking features of the last three decades, those of neoliberal hegemony, is the way in which 'the economic' has been removed from the sphere of politico-ideological contestation. This was central to the establishment of a singular narrative and its ineluctability. It was central to Thatcher's TINA, as it was to Blair's narrative of modernisation (which could only take one form), and it is now the anchor for Osborne's pronouncements as he slices back the public sector that he really doesn't want to do this, but there is no choice but to bow before economic necessity. All, of course, are assertions, meant to staple down a particular common sense. There are always political alternatives.

One response to this argument in relation to the current austerity is that it is not necessary, it is ideological. And this is correct so far as it goes. But it also needs to go further. One aspect of the ideological formation being referred to in such a response is neoliberalism. Indeed the whole period of hegemony that succeeded the dissolution of the post-war social-democratic settlement is often referred to as 'neoliberal'. I have many times done this myself, and I agree with Stuart Hall's argument about this in Chapter 1. But even in specific reference to the economic, this is a characterisation that must come with a host of caveats. For one thing, insofar as 'neoliberal' describes a stance in relation to economic policy, it has over the last thirty years been a doctrine conspicuous by its selective use, brought out to legitimise privatisations and cuts to public services, for instance; quietly ignored when it would not serve dominant interests.[2] When capital itself needs state intervention or subsidy – from infrastructure, to the bail-out of the banks, to the requirements of the South East of England – the rubrics of neoliberalism are ignored. And this is the further point: what this mobilisation of a particular economic theory is really about is playing to particular interests. The response to the assertion of the unavoidable necessity of the cuts, then, is not just that they are ideological, but that they are meant to serve certain interests as opposed to others. The contest in the end, whether or not this becomes politically visible, is between the interests of different social groups – which takes us to the heart of whether or not this current dislocation can be turned into a moment of real conjunctural rupture.

So this is crucial. Without challenging the idea that the economic is some kind of external force we cannot change the terms of debate about it. Within this, perhaps the crucial founding assumption is that markets are natural, market forces a force of nature. The degree to which this is inscribed in common sense is astonishing. This is true both in the small negotiations of the daily lives of individuals whose very imaginations have been financialised and in the grand conti-nental sweep as 'the markets' roam Europe dragooning economy after economy into policies of their own choosing. That markets are natural is now so embedded in the structure of thought that even the fact that it is an assumption is rarely brought to light. It is, of course, not a new common sense. Karl Polanyi in *The Great Transformation* raged bril-liantly against it, both at the level of individual behaviour and at the level of society. But it does seem at the moment peculiarly startling and pervasive.[3]

One reason for this lies in the structural dominance of the financial sector within the economy. On the one hand the very nature of finance chimes with the times – its apparent immateriality, its apparent light-ness and disembeddedness, its ease of global flow, its character of pure exchange, the individualistic character of its 'production' process. In all of this finance fits the ideological moment (if in a distorted and distorting way). So challenging the dominance of finance within the economy and geography of this country (which is anyway necessary) could mean also challenging some deeply woven elements in the hege-monic imagination. But finance chimes with the times precisely because it plays into other developments, in ideology and culture, that have been happening independently. All those challenges raised in the 1960s and subsequently to the classic characteristics of the social-democratic settlement have been crucial here. The emphasis on flexibility, differentiation, movement rather than stasis, on the indi-vidual rather than the preconstituted group – all these independent developments, subverted and subsumed into a capitalist framework to be sure, have in turn proved fertile ground within which the ideolog-ical underpinnings of speculative finance could flourish and take popular hold.

TAKING A LEAP

Challenging the terms of this ideological dominance implies a step change in political debate, including the terms of debate over the economy. It means attacking from somewhere else entirely. For instance, challenging the assumed naturalness of markets – even pointing out that this *is* an assumption – means going beyond social democracy in its current formulation. 'Social democracy' has meant many things over its lifetime, but crucial to its present imaginary is a formulation that it is necessary to intervene in markets in order to ameliorate their sometimes noxious effects. But this gives the whole game away from the beginning. It accepts the imagination of markets as 'out there', and of social actors, such as governments, as intervening in this external force. (This, of course, is precisely the opposite of Polanyi's formulation.) To challenge this would change the imagination of the economy: not natural force and intervention but a whole variety of social relations that need some kind of coordination.

This kind of leap is what is needed. At the moment the bulk of public debate takes place on terrain marked out by Tories and New Labour. An ideological challenge should be about redefining this political field, establishing our own terrain, and thus bringing about a (re)definition of political frontiers, clearer and sharper and about what kind of society, and whose interests, we stand for. *That* might be worth fighting for.

What follows is a brief introduction to three potential areas of engagement.

What is the economy for?

First, in response to the usual terminally boring questions that restrict the imagination to, basically, what we have now, we could respond with a bigger question: 'What is an economy *for*?'[4] As already noted, even Cameron has mused that what matters is more than GDP. The trouble is that most of the people voicing such thoughts seem to be in search of something warm and cuddly to *add on to* 'the economic'. In fact what should be at issue are the forms of organisation, the orientation and the priorities, of the economic itself. What kind of economy do we want? What do we want it to provide?

There is in fact lots of work around on alternative models for the UK economy (see, for instance, new economics foundation, New

Political Economy Group, the Green New Deal, etc). There is no shortage of ideas. The constant onslaught of denial that anyone has any alternative to offer is (i) wrong (ii) part of the political strategy of asserting necessity and (iii) a reflection of the general difficulty in gaining public purchase for ideas from the left.

One of the reasons for this difficulty in gaining traction is that to the extent that ideas from the left do get a hearing they tend to (have to) be argued on the political terrain of existing economic policy. The unthought common sense remains undisturbed; it is not brought up from its deep sedimentation in the accepted terms of the social, to be made political in the sense of challengeable. It is this nature of the framing argument that has to be questioned. What if we were to start somewhere else?

What if we did ask what an economy is for? What if we brought to centre-stage issues of care, for instance, and its current undervaluing? This would certainly touch upon the discontents in the current structure of feeling. It would raise the question of why, if we all say we value these qualities so much, they are so deprioritised and underpaid. It would speak to women, currently being hit hardest by the cuts. It is a positive argument for sections of the public sector. It would make the ideas for different economic models more comprehensible, for they would be set in a different ideological field. Even in current economic terms there is the argument that the multiplier effects of investment in care are more likely to stay local, and certainly to be, regionally, more evenly distributed than those of investment in almost any other sector. But most of all it would set the question of the economic in a different ideological field, and a different prioritisation of values. Similar kinds of argument can be made for prioritising ecological sustainability.

Bringing such ideas together with a challenge to the assumption of the naturalness of markets also brings down that other element of the hegemonic economic imaginary: that curious sequentialism which demands that first we grow the economy and then we redistribute. In fact, there are different models of 'growth' itself, with very different distributional implications (even a cursory comparison of, say, the Wilson and Thatcher periods will demonstrate that). Such a reorientation also provides a frame in which expenditure and regulation can be seen as positives, as part of building a society. It can encourage the thinking of society as a whole and, in some manner, as collective (like that notion of the NHS as collective insurance, as one element in the construction of a public).

Equality and liberty

A second area of engagement – and an element that will surely be present in any left answer to the question 'what is an economy for' – is equality.

'Liberal democracy' is the product of an articulation between two different traditions – 'the liberal tradition constituted by the rule of law, the defence of human rights and the respect [for] individual liberty' and 'the democratic tradition whose main ideas are those of equality, identity between governing and governed and popular sovereignty.'[5] As Mouffe points out, there is an inherent conflict between the respective logics of these two traditions. Any particular social settlement, therefore, reflects the particular form of articulation between the two that has achieved hegemony.

I would argue that one absolutely crucial but perhaps not so often noted element in the shift between social settlements, from the postwar social-democratic settlement to the one we call neoliberal, has been a major change in the nature of this articulation. Basically, equality has lost out, hands down, to liberalism.

The simple increases in economic inequality under the present settlement are one indication of this. New Labour's pathological inability to refer to redistribution is another. Then there is the rise to prominence of discourses of individual choice (tied up with the general rubbishing of collectivism – see later), and even of discourses of multiculturalism in place of (though they did not have to be in place of) those of class. There is the prioritisation of electoral form over political substance. Archer captures it brilliantly in relation to the general election in the UK:

> *The Guardian* made the remarkable claim – on the 1 of May no less – that the central issue of the election was reform of the electoral system ... the idea that in the middle of the biggest economic crisis since the 1930s, the demand for electoral reform should be the defining issue is quite extraordinary. Here we are, saddled with huge debts that will force major cuts – in jobs, benefits, pensions, and living standards – on totally blameless fellow citizens, and the great question of moment is ... electoral reform![6]

Absolutely. And the same attitudes are evident at international level, where a rhetoric of 'democracy' has become a cover for an exclusive focus on liberalism: Western governments' readings of developments in other countries (from China to Venezuela) focus exclusively on evaluations of their 'democratic' status (evaluations that are often wildly wrong) and ignore all else, even when huge progress has been made in relieving poverty. Likewise the interpretation of recent events in North Africa and the Middle East has been moulded entirely around 'getting rid of (selected) dictators'. The seething discontent over poverty and unemployment is erased from the picture. In spite of the terminology of democracy that is brandished in all these instances, it is actually *liberalism* that is being prioritised; these discourses in fact say little about the real content of the democratic tradition among whose main principles is that of equality.

This shift from equality to liberalism is at the core of the change that has taken place in the articulation of the economic and the ideological. It is central to the shift from the post-war settlement to the current one. Indeed, neoliberalism represents a threat to democratic institutions.[7] And vice versa. Addressing this shift would raise again the question of what an economy is for. It might also help us focus on the much-noted divorce, within the left constituency, between the working class and the (so-called) progressive middle class.[8]

Collectivity

A third area of engagement is collectivity – the loss of which is among the many aspects of the ideological that one might address. This loss has happened both in terms of collectivity as a material form and in terms of collectivity as a legitimate part of the political imaginary; and it represents a further symptom of the increasing dominance of individualism, which is of course itself part of the shift towards liberalism.

It is evident in a thousand ways. Take, for instance, the Lib Dems. It is common to hear excoriation of the economic liberals within their party, coupled with a warmth towards 'social liberals'. But while the social liberals might be in favour of many freedoms and indeed of greater equality, they conceive of these things in individualist terms and deride any collective means of getting there. In the roundtable discussion in *Soundings* 45, Stuart Hall observed that 'the Lib Dems are more progressive. But they are more progressive, not more to the left', and he points out that the party 'has always been about the private individual, individualism'.[9] It is extremely important that this is recognised. (It resonates too, of course, with the shift from equality to liberalism, discussed above.) To mention again an author referred to earlier: it is worth returning to Polanyi's discussion of the suppression of 'combinations' in the nineteenth century. There was much talk then too about relieving poverty, but a simultaneous suppression of the poor's own means of political action. Lib-Dem and New Labour discourse is effectively a way of bringing about the same result, not by law but by dismissal from the popular imaginary of collective action (especially by trade unions). *The Guardian*'s famous hostile editorial response to Len McCluskey was a real high (low) point of this. Sympathy for the poor is allowed, as is (very effective) documentation of poverty, but it must – for these commentators – be addressed by legislation proposed by them and absolutely not by the collective self-organisation, especially into trades unions, of people themselves.[10] The form of collectivity is changing, and indeed must change. New types of collective organising are emerging. They are essential to the achievement of political goals and to the changing of political consciousness.

CONCLUSION

Referring to Labour before the last national election, when they already knew they had lost, Hall has argued that they had two choices: 'One was to move in a decisively different direction and perhaps be out of power for quite a long time but to build an alternative hegemony. And the other was to play on within the neoliberal terrain, and they chose the latter'.[11] This is the kind of leap that I was arguing for above, and, as I have also argued, getting out of the neoliberal terrain is a matter of the ideological as well as the economic. Maybe Ed Miliband, in insisting on taking his time, and on reframing arguments, is embarking on this. Certainly all those hostile voices urging speed are also a pressure to keep it superficial – yet more 'policies' within the same ideological ballpark. Certainly, too, the Labour Party will find significant shifts difficult to make without pressure from outside the party, and here the emergence of a host of grassroots voices gives some hope. What is certain is the need to redefine the political field across that crucial intersection between the ideological and the economic, and in favour of different social interests. Only then might a serious shift in the social balance of power be on the cards.

NOTES

1. See Hall and Massey in Chapter 4. This chapter also draws on the more general analysis by Massey, and the roundtable discussion, in *Soundings* issue 45.
2. D. Massey, 'The political struggle ahead', Chapter 5.
3. There is a strange irony here. In the past world (in the UK) of material production, the left had to force the imagination of the enemy beyond the person/owner/capitalist to 'the system'. Now it is depersonalised, and definitely the system, but it is acquiesced in as ineluctable – in such a way that it is difficult to see the interests at stake.
4. Some of the ideas in this section draw on the excellent discussions in the New Political Economy Group (new-political-economy-network@googlegroups.com).
5. C. Mouffe, *The democratic paradox*, Verso 2005, pp2-3.
6. R. Archer, 'Leading Labour', Guest Editorial, *Renewal* 19.1, spring 2011, p8.
7. *The democratic paradox*, p6 (see note 5).
8. There is no space to go into this here, but as I write Ed Miliband is being bombarded by New Labour opponents and Mandelsonian policy groups, their voices magnified by the liberal (precisely) press, to listen to the feelings of the southern suburbs. Entirely in responsive mode, this admits no possibility of politicians *changing* the political scene (see again the excellent piece by Archer – note 6). Even more importantly, it is an argument about individual policies (a bribe here, a bribe there – no question of taking a leap), rather than the construction of an alternative vision, of a different kind of society, that might take hold more widely.
9. S. Davison, S. Hall, M. Rustin and J. Rutherford, 'Labour in a time of coalition', *Soundings* 45, summer 2010, pp19, 20.
10. There are exceptions to the non-recognition of collectivity, the prime one these days being London Citizens. But LC is itself antitrades union in much of its spokespersons' pronouncements, and is also riven with political problems (as are trade unions) which should be addressed more publicly. The trade unions are constantly attacked for *their* perceived deficiencies. London Citizens, by contrast, is idealised.
11. 'Labour in a time of coalition', p30 (see note 9).

NOTES ON CONTRIBUTORS

John Clarke is Emeritus Professor of Social Policy and Criminology at the Open University.

Sally Davison is co-editor of *Soundings*.

Stuart Hall was a founding editor of *Soundings* and a regular contributor to *Marxism Today*.

Doreen Massey was one of the founding editors of *Soundings* and is currently Emeritus Professor of Geography at the Open University.

Michael Rustin was one of the founding editors of *Soundings* and is currently Professor of Sociology at the University of East London.

After Neoliberalism:

THE KILBURN MANIFESTO

Stuart Hall, Doreen Massey & Michael Rustin (eds)

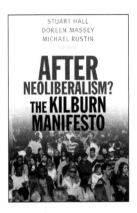

'*The Kilburn Manifesto is a* fitting testament to the contribution of Stuart Hall to British political life. It presents an incisive and powerful analysis of the current neoliberal moment making it essential reading for anyone interested not only in understanding the present but also in developing strategies for intervening into it.'

Professor Alan Finlayson, University of East Anglia

This book brings together in one volume contributions made to the public debate around the Kilburn Manifesto, a *Soundings* project first launched in spring 2013. The manifesto seeks to map the political, economic, social and cultural contours of neoliberalism. Each chapter analyses a specific issue or theme, with chapters on the economy, race, class, gender and generation under neoliberalism. The aim is to call into question the neoliberal order itself, and find radical alternatives to its foundational assumptions.

Publication date: February 2015

ISBN 9781910448106
Price: £12.99

To order, visit www.lwbooks.co.uk